P9-DVU-588

One Day I Wrote Back

Interacting with Scripture through Creative Writing

JANE HERRING

UPPER ROOM BOOKS®
NASHVILLE

ONE DAY I WROTE BACK: Interacting with Scripture through Creative Writing
Copyright © 2015 by Jane Herring
All rights reserved.

No part of this book may be reproduced in any manner whatsoever without written permission of the publisher except in the case of brief quotations embodied in critical articles or reviews. For information, write Upper Room Books, 1908 Grand Avenue, Nashville, Tennessee 37212.

Upper Room Books® website: books.upperroom.org

UPPER ROOM®, UPPER ROOM BOOKS®, and design logos are trademarks owned by The Upper Room®, a Ministry of GBOD®, Nashville, Tennessee. All rights reserved.

All scripture quotations are from the New Revised Standard Version Bible, copyright © 1989 the Division of Christian Education of the National Council of the Churches of Christ in the United States of America. Used by permission. All rights reserved.

Cover design and hand-lettering: Kristi Smith / Juicebox Designs
Interior design: Kristin Goble / PerfecType

ISBN 978-0-8358-1375-4 (print)
ISBN 978-0-8358-1376-1 (mobi)
ISBN 978-0-8358-1377-8 (epub)

Printed in the United States of America

∽

For Victor, for whom so many are grateful.

For fellow believers asking for help in their unbelief.

And for Stan with all my love.

∽

Contents

One Day I Wrote Back

O ver the course of my childhood and youth spent in the "Bible Belt," I often heard people say, "This scripture really speaks to me." Well, scripture did not speak to me. Preachers, teachers, friends, radio, and the television spoke to me. The Bible awed and frightened me. Its amazing stories and poetic passages intrigued me, but the strangeness and gruesomeness of other passages left me more than a little concerned and confused about God and humanity.

In my elementary school years, I discovered Old Testament stories through Sunday school, and I loved them. The gentle animals herded lovingly by Noah onto the ark, Joseph's magnificently-colored coat, and Moses' grand gesture through which God parted the Red Sea—these stories delighted my sense of drama. By middle school, I read the Bible on my own. Imagine my surprise when I encountered other stories: Lot and his daughters, the concubine cut into twelve pieces, the various images of a vicious and angry God. The New Testament seemed to depict a more loving God in Jesus Christ, but even parts of Jesus' gospel appeared more threatening and exclusive than loving and liberating.

Though the Bible was the single most prominent text of my youth, I had a love-hate relationship with it that took years for me to understand. Christianity and the Bible were such strong influences on the culture where I lived, and I could not imagine anywhere in the world where people weren't constantly discussing God. Nor could I imagine the range and variety of Christian faith, thought, and practice that existed throughout history and the world. In my own environment—the rural South of the 1970s and 80s—I felt limited on how much questioning would be tolerated, even among more open-minded and educated believers.

What most people told me scripture said to them sounded a lot more like the culture talking than God speaking. On television, people invoked God to damn certain souls to hell. God seemed angry and hateful and only approved of a handful of persons and behaviors. Fear and worry accompanied this depiction of God, as did judgment, disapproval, punishment, and shame. Sin was so often discussed, I could not tell if God wanted to help free humanity from sin or relished punishing us like a bloodthirsty dictator.

My private experiences of God communicated overwhelming feelings of love and a solid sense of trust and well-being, as if God really was there for me when I felt alone, confused, or lost. I had a series of dreams in which everyone I knew came together and acted kindly toward one another. People who had been cruel to me or to others, people who played large or small roles in my life—everyone was there at this great party-like event, laughing and having fun. Though God did not make an appearance, God was the reason for the party. God created the happy, forgiving atmosphere. This joyful feeling is how I thought of God, and all too often, it did not resemble the fearful and judgmental portrait of God drawn by traveling preachers, televangelists, and even some people in my community.

In my small, Southern town, poverty was pervasive. Racism, classism, and sexism created invisible forces that ordered much of the social interaction in my childhood. Scripture was used to bolster those who had a vested interest in how things *ought* to go—how races *ought* to relate, how women and men *ought* to behave, who *ought* to dominate financially, who *ought* to get away with breaking laws, and who *ought* to be prosecuted to the fullest extent of the law. The use of the Bible to justify societal and cultural norms ultimately made me wonder if the Bible was either too complicated a book to understand in any meaningful way or too slippery a book to actually mean anything at all. I was not confident enough in my youth to feel comfortable with the questions I had about the Bible and the various theologies I encountered.

Some men and women in my life spoke about scripture with an insight and relationship to the Word that I knew to be deep and real. Through their guidance, I encountered a God who desires liberation and freedom from oppression for all creation. They exemplified for me what it looks like to live in service to others. These voices tended to be softer and more honest about the darkness dwelling in their own hearts and less certain in claiming to know what God was thinking or doing. Even with these examples of kind, religious people, I doubted my identity as a Christian and my ability to interact with the Bible.

In college I studied the literary aspects of the Bible—its correlation to the works of Shakespeare and other masterful classics and its themes and various styles of narrative and poetry. I found I could connect with the Bible through studying history, learning what I could about the ancient history represented in the Old Testament and about first-century Palestine. Through history and reason, I began to understand some of the stories and situations in the Bible that had once seemed unrelated to my experience. The people of the Bible struggled with the same fears, feelings, longings, and desires with which we struggle today. God's people were not perfect, and God loved them anyway. After years of trying to cultivate my spiritual life, leaving and returning to the church, and holding my own as best I could with the Bible, I matriculated into Vanderbilt Divinity School for a Master of Divinity. Many of my fellow students found the historical, academic approach to the Bible challenging to their faiths. Watching their disillusionment and struggles was painful, particularly as I found myself drawn further into a life of faith through this tension between faith and reason.

Still, scripture did not really speak to me until one day I wrote back. On a Saturday afternoon, one of my professors invited a small group of us to practice a form of *lectio divina*— careful reading of scripture coupled with silent contemplation. He instructed us to take up pen and write back to scripture in whatever form inspired us: poetry, lists, story, letter, and so on. He called this practice *scriptio divina*, a term he had learned from the writings of Stephanie Paulsell.

When I began interacting with scripture though writing, a new relationship unfolded. I copied scripture word for word, questioning it, prodding the text to uncover what had not been said, speaking back to it about what I found confusing, too good to be true, too hard, too easy, and sometimes trying to rewrite it with details from contemporary life. In this way, I entered into a relationship with scripture. Faith and the Spirit—both mysterious—sustained me through early adulthood, reason opened the door to the Bible, and now imagination exercised through creative writing forged a living relationship to the Bible. I no longer allowed myself to be the page upon which others wrote their hopes, fears, thoughts, and dreams about the Sacred. I wrote back.

As I began speaking to scripture, it began to speak to me. I am not saying that I started receiving answers to all of life's problems. I still worried about being a good enough person.

Past mistakes or hurts still bothered me. I still wondered where God was during painful experiences. But I truly felt in conversation with God while I took part in my own spiritual growth and understanding. I found myself drawn further into the mystery of Christian faith, further away from certitude, and closer to a life with scripture I had always longed for but had not believed possible. I discovered room in my relationship with God for faith, reason, and imagination. For me, a fuller life with God requires all three.

Some time after I began practicing *scriptio divina*, one of my professors, a practicing member of a Jewish Orthodox synagogue, said something that confirmed the importance of this kind of creative engagement with scripture. As an aside to a lecture one day, she said that the Jewish community did not value consensus about biblical matters the way many Christians do. She gave a brief description of *midrash*—the ancient art of inquiry used to discover meaning in the Hebrew Bible—and went on to say that argument and conversation are key elements in Jewish religious life. Suddenly Jesus at the Temple arguing his point of view took on a whole new meaning. I felt invited to argue, to speak back, to be part of the conversation that was already taking place in the Living Word. If the Bible is indeed the Living Word, what is more lively than the give-and-take of conversation? If the Bible is God's sacred word, what would be more fitting than to engage all our God-given faculties—intellect and imagination—in our relationship with it?

I use this technique of writing back to scripture as a personal spiritual practice, in my work as a chaplain, when preparing sermons, and at contemplative retreats. Interacting with scripture in this way never fails to open new and refreshing ways to see human experience as part of the still unfolding story of creation. I am reminded of Jesus as he challenged interpretations of scripture and walked with the sick, the poor, the outcast, the wealthy, the Jews and Gentiles, men and women.

He wanted to show them abundant life in God, eternal and yet always new. When I hear about *midrash*, I am reminded that Jesus came of age in an environment that valued productive argumentation, inquiry, questioning, interpreting, and reinter- preting. I believe it is our responsibility as believers to engage scripture critically and creatively and to use this creative and questioning approach to our lives.

I've known many believers in different stages of their faith journeys who have taken up *scriptio divina*. Some have had long, rich relationships with the Bible; some only read the Bible on occasion. Some were raised as Christians but do not con- sider themselves currently religious; some consider themselves Christian but have had bad experiences with organized religion in general and churches in particular. Some are very active in church but would not want to be left alone in a room to pray or read the Bible. I've witnessed some of the most moving expe- riences with *scriptio divina* through people who claim atheism or agnosticism and have not picked up a Bible in years. I share these varied experiences with you because I hope you will feel encouraged to take up these exercises no matter where you are in your journey.

I, and those with whom I have worked, have responded to scripture in beautiful journals, in cheap composition books, on the backs of hospital admittance papers, on Kleenex boxes, on napkins, on receipts, and in the margins of many church bul- letins. We have sat at candlelit tables in delicious silence. We have written on buses and subways. We have written in hos- pital beds and in psychiatric wards, in pre-op surgical holding bays, at picnic tables, and under shady trees. I have compared notes with people as we cherished a weeklong retreat and as we hurriedly exchanged emails regarding our private writing. I have written some responses to scripture which were too private or painful, too wild or too precious to share. In fact, I threw some of mine into a fire pit. Nevertheless, I invite you to join us. Be bold and use this book in a way that suits you. Do not hold yourself back in these exercises—you are welcome to share your words, keep them private, or throw them away as you see fit.

Separation from God will always be a part of the human condition. We live in a broken world, and we are flawed, even though the spark of the Creator resides within us. Throughout my faith journey, I've worked to get past problematic portions of the Bible. Writing my way into scripture has become one of the ways I stay alive spiritually, in Christ, in conversation with God. It keeps me honest about my own life and my experience. Again, separation is a given, and our journeys in life are, even at their best, not perfect. We will encounter failure, hard-heartedness, injury, self-doubt, and disappointment. I have come to understand that my salvation was worked out over two thousand years ago, but my journey of responding to and living into God's grace is happening here and now, broken as this world may be.

The beauty and brokenness of the world is not new. We see persons in the Bible responding to and questioning God over and over again. Remember Job who did not hold back his questions and his painful lament. Remember Moses who argued with God about whether he was the right man to lead the Israelites. Remember Sarah who laughed, Gideon who challenged God, Jacob who wrestled, and Mary who sang. Even though we must each work out our own relationships with God—each of us alone in the depths of our beings with questions, thoughts, and personal experience—as we put pen to paper, we are not alone.

How to Use This Book

This book is about forging a fresh, personal, creative relationship with the Bible. You will cultivate ways to write about the questions and epiphanies you experience about life, God, yourself, and others. Spending time with and writing about the Bible will spark these epiphanies. Through this book, you are embarking on an adventure, and even if you do the same exercises over and over, you are not likely to write the same thing twice.

You may find these exercises useful for a small-group study, as a supplement to a prayer meeting, as the basis for a weekend retreat, or as a guide for a personal daily practice. This book could be used for a new group just forming or as a resource for a longstanding group. In the Leader's Guide, I offer ideas about how to use this resource in the contexts listed above and in others.

Do not expect "This passage means . . ." guidance from this book. I hope you will hold the Bible close as you work through the exercises, but you will write *out of* the Bible and *in response to* the Bible. In your writing, your primary goal will be to mine your personal responses to the Bible. In a way, the Bible serves as inspiration for you to uncover your thoughts, questions, suspicions, secrets, and longings with regard to God, your faith, the Bible, and life. In this approach to relating to the Bible, feel free to use whatever you know, whatever you feel, whatever you question, whatever you suspect or can imagine. I am not advocating an overthrow of your religious heritage or culture. I am suggesting that through writing with the Bible in a free and unfettered way, you can deepen your own sensitivity to God's presence in your life and to your own spiritual development.

In seminary I learned about "the way of God's Fresh Address." In this understanding of the authority of the Bible, the thoughts and images from contemporary life that the Bible brings to mind are just as relevant as the original, ancient context of the Bible. For instance, when reading about Samson and Delilah, you may find yourself writing about your first haircut and how vulnerable, grown-up, or awkward you felt afterward. This memory may call to mind an anger you have held against your mother, causing you to reflect on Samson's relationship with his mother. You may go back and reread earlier parts of his story. You may ultimately end up wondering about Delilah, about God, about the people caught under the fallen roof of the place where Samson was held. This may cause you to ask questions about where God is in this story, where God is when a stadium full of people collapses, where God is when you are led astray by loving people who are not good for you. Or you may never move past that memory of you in the chair at the salon, your hair falling in ribbons to the floor.

A Word about Difficulties

The goal of *scriptio divina* is to interact with the Bible and to do so on your own terms, with no one else's expectations or beliefs in mind. You need not be concerned with spelling, punctuation, capitalization, or any of the grammatical issues that require attention when writing for a particular purpose or audience. Free yourself from any rules or regulations that may cause you distress.

You may have trouble getting started with your writing. Let yourself be messy, sloppy, and totally imperfect. You are not writing with the goal of showing what you have written to others. You are not writing with the finished product in mind. You are writing for the sake of experiencing the thoughts and feelings that come as you put words on the page. If you happen to end up with some writing that becomes a short story, essay, or novel, great! If you mine your writing at a later time for use in Sunday school lessons, articles, poems, hymns, or any other form of writing, well, that's wonderful. But that is not the goal of this book.

Use the reflection and writing prompts as starting points, but feel free to develop your own techniques. Make lists of words that appeal to you from the passage. Make a list of the wishes or fears the passage calls to mind. Choose a line from the passage that strikes you in some particular way and write it over and over. The Leader's Guide offers other ideas as well, but your guiding principle is to write. There is no wrong way. You are not meant to come up with a particular product. The experience of writing serves as your measure of success.

Difficult Thoughts and Feelings

From time to time writing brings up difficult or uncomfortable thoughts. You may question long held beliefs. You may find your own thoughts do not line up with those around you. You may find yourself asking questions you have never asked before or questions to which there are no easy answers.

When you encounter such thoughts, feelings, or questions, the best step is to pray. Pray to the loving God who created you and ask God to help you deal with whatever you experienced in your writing. Learning to live with questions and to hold yourself and these questions mercifully is a worthy endeavor and very much a possibility as you write with the Bible in this way. Accepting the flow of thoughts and feelings that are stirred up as I read the Bible has given me greater resilience and joy and deepened my relationship with God.

If you are using this book in a group, you will need to decide whether or not to share your difficult thoughts or feelings with others in the group (more on that in the Leader's Guide). Each member of the group has to judge his or her ability and willingness to be vulnerable and the level of trust present in the group. If you find it too uncomfortable to sit with difficult feelings, seek help from someone you trust—a pastor, counselor, or friend. Pastoral counselors are trained counselors who focus on the integrating psychotherapy and spirituality. A pastoral counselor can offer a safe place to discuss wide-ranging issues that involve both the spirit and the psyche. Twelve-step groups can also be helpful. There are 12-step groups for many issues. Having a place to speak and learn from others who are using a spiritually-based program to deal with life's difficulties can be invaluable.

A Word about the Chapters

I arranged this book thematically. I chose themes that I've seen surface repeatedly in people's lives as I served as a pastor, spiritual guide, and chaplain. These themes by no means exhaust the issues touched upon in the Bible. However, as I meet and work with people in various life stages, I almost always encounter those in need of healing, sustenance in the course of life's journey, and meaningful life experiences. Many long for the sense that God is present in their lives, question their abilities to relate to others and to God, and feel as though they have gone astray. Some scripture passages listed in this book are old friends of mine and some are new. Even as I write this book, I am getting to know some parts of scripture on a deeper level by using *scriptio divina*.

A reflection follows each verse. These essays are not intended as examples of the writing practice described in the book. The essays are, however, creative rather than instructional or professional. In writing the essays, I used the same free associative method I encourage you to use. If specific knowledge of the text or time period was part of my general knowledge, I used it, but I did not attempt to write a definitive commentary on the scriptural passage. The essays serve to suggest one of many directions one might go when reading, reflecting, and writing on the scripture.

Enough about the book, what it is and what it is not. I hope, above all, that it can become a friend to you on your journey of faith. I hope it inspires you to seek a relationship with the

Bible, a relationship in which you feel free to speak and think creatively. Speaking authentically about you life nourishes the soul—your own and others'. You can speak authentically to God and about yourself through this writing practice.

I offer this guiding prayer as you begin interacting with scripture through creative writing:

> *Holy Spirit, open my imagination and allow me to find a safe space within to explore myself and your holy Word. Guide me with the assurance that I am loved, that you desire goodness for humanity, and that your grace abounds even in the most difficult circumstances. Give me the resilience, God, to face joy and sorrow, to take responsibility for my faith, and ultimately to hand all my life over to you. Amen.*

1

Healing and Restoration

Humans experience the need for healing in so many ways. We may experience serious illness or other types of personal loss. We may experience them alone or corporately as a couple or a family, as a nation, as a community, as a city, or as a church. As many ways to experience loss and the need for healing exist as ways to be human, in both the individual as well as the collective sense. The selections in this chapter address the need for healing and the quest for restoration after trauma. These three listings are but a few of the passages we could explore from the Bible, but they are some of my favorites.

Not Too Proud to Heal
2 Kings 5:1-16

This passage is as fraught with drama and intrigue as any work by William Shakespeare, William Faulkner, or any television drama. Read the passage once to get a sense of the event depicted, then imagine with me that the events are taking place in the twenty-first century.

Let's say it's the year 2005, and Donald Rumsfeld has contracted an unbelievably bad case of eczema that no doctor can cure. His wife tells him that their housekeeper mentioned that he could be healed by the woman who lives beside a chapel in Chimayo, New Mexico, a tiny town in the middle of the desert. In desperation, Rumsfeld goes to New Mexico for this healing.

Inexplicably, instead of going to see the healer the housekeeper told him to see, he asks President Bush to write a letter to New Mexico's governor (who just happens to be a Democrat), Bill Richardson. The letter tells Richardson to heal Rumsfeld.

When he receives the letter, Richardson goes on a tirade about how the President of the United States is trying to make him look like a fool so he'll lose his office. Somehow the woman in Chimayo is aware of what is going on and sends word for Rumsfeld to come to her.

Rumsfeld arrives at the healer's doorstep in the middle of the New Mexican desert in a caravan of shiny black cars carrying bars of gold from the Federal Reserve and bags of clothing from Neiman Marcus. Just as he reaches the door of her house, a barefooted child runs outside and says her mother is busy but Rumsfeld should bathe in the Rio Grande and be healed.

I think Rumsfeld would react to the healer's nonchalance about the same way Naaman reacted to Elisha's message. Rumsfeld knows who he is; he knows his station in life. How much more important and successful is Donald Rumsfeld than a poor woman in a desolate town in New Mexico? How much more important is Naaman than Elisha? And Elisha cannot be bothered to not show up and give Naaman an elaborate magic show of healing?

When Naaman reacts badly to Elisha's messenger, it is his servants who know how to talk to him, stressing Naaman's ability to perform massively complicated tasks and persuading him that this simple task Elisha gives him is all the more manageable. The servants know how to draw Naaman's attention away from his success and stature and help him focus on his desire to be healed. The servants—who are not even named in this story—ensure Naaman's healing.

Naaman goes to the Jordan—a river that is just a creek in comparison to the magnificent rivers of Naaman's homeland—and he bathes in the water seven times, just as instructed. And he emerges with skin like a child, made new, healed.

No matter our station in life, we must humble ourselves and open our hearts in order to receive healing. Some of us do not stumble on our pride the way Naaman does. Sometimes we are the ones in need of healing, and sometimes we are the servants called to speak a guiding word. Neither of these roles is easy.

Listening to others when we've gotten lost in our own egos—lost in how important we are or even how inferior we may feel—often proves difficult. If we are open to being healed, however, we may hear the encouragement of others to move forward in faith and humility.

If we find ourselves relating to the servant's position more, we see that speaking up without worldly authority, class status, or name to impart credibility may prove difficult. The servant speaks through faith and care for Naaman. Allowing words to come from the heart of God's hope and healing can be daunting. Feelings of inferiority often block the flow of wisdom and healing God wants to offer the world through us.

Though the servants act as key agents in this story, I do not want to gloss over the fact that slavery—various forms of indentured servitude and human trafficking—remains a very real problem in the world today. We find no grace in an ideology that allows slavery, supports the belief that some people do not get names, or asserts that some bodies are worth more than others. God offers salvation from oppression for both the oppressed and the oppressor. Through God's guidance, we can free ourselves from the darkness that binds us and prevents us from seeing others as equal, loved children of God. This story belongs as much to Naaman's wife's servant as to Naaman. When God gives her a word to say, she knows to whom she belongs: to God, not to Naaman.

When I ground myself in my God-given identity—a beloved child of God—and not in my station in life, I too can speak up. I can say the words of the unnamed slave girl. I can take the hand of a friend in distress and say, "Look, there might be another way." The slave girl did not think of herself as a slave. As God's servant, she spoke out of conviction not enslavement. We can learn from her bold actions.

At first, Namaan was too proud to see this offer of healing and restoration, but he was able to put his ego aside and receive the help he needed. We can do this as well.

Read the passage again, once or twice more.

REFLECTION QUESTIONS

1. When have you needed healing in body or spirit? What was your affliction? How were you similar to Naaman in your hope to be healed? How were you different?

2. Who are the nameless people in your life, and how does your life intersect with theirs? In what aspects of life are you nameless?

3. Where have you seen a story like Naaman's play out in life, literature, or art? What observations can you make about power, prophesy, class, status, and faith?

4. Why does God heal Naaman, a warrior from a foreign land? What does this act say about God's view of foreigners?

WRITING EXERCISES

1. Rewrite the 1 Kings passage from the perspective of the servant. Give her a name and tell her story.

2. Rewrite the passage from the perspective of Naaman's wife. What is your investment in seeing him healed? How do you feel when he comes home and tells you he is now worshiping a foreign God?

3. Write about the healing and restoration you have experienced in your own life.

4. Write a letter to the Aramean king from the perspective of the King of Israel. Does the King of Israel really believe in his own prophet's healing power? What does this mean to the King of Israel's political power?

Restoration Promised

Isaiah 66:10-12

In the scripture reading, Isaiah depicts a glorious future of Israel redeemed, purified, and brought back to glory after devastation. Restoration, though, presupposes destruction. Destruction means living through pain and loss and possibly guilt and shame as well. I try to avoid these feelings and experiences. I learned from an early age to keep the exterior of my life looking good, and I suffered greatly when I was unable to do so. I learned to ignore the pain that I was in and the pain other people experienced—from personal slights to larger societal problems.

Being able to carry on during a hard time with head held high is a good trait. Knowing that many of life's problems cannot be "fixed" but must be endured is also good. But building a fortress around our minds and hearts and denying the difficulty of life can be harmful. Doing so creates a fog in which days pass and we are never truly aware of what is going on in our lives.

Part of my tendency toward avoidance is probably due to the time and place from which I come—a middle-class girl from the rural South born in the late 1960s. I find some truth in the persona of the stereotypical Southern woman who uses denial as the bedrock of good manners. When faced with an upsetting reality, a Southern woman does not even acknowledge it because, my dear, it simply is not occurring—a perfectly appropriate response when the local gossips are baiting you about why your daddy is not in church but tragic when an entire community ignores the recurring bruises and broken bones of a vulnerable child.

Denial serves as a coping mechanism when life becomes too painful. The danger in coping mechanisms lies in their ability to work effectively for a few years but then to take on lives of their own. When we deny destructive trends in a relationship, our coping mechanisms protect us from feeling hurt. On the flip side, we cannot make healthy changes that will lead to lives of deeper meaning, fuller relationships, and more caring communities if we are numb to the problems of our present lives. Worse yet, destructive trends that go unnoticed can worsen until difficult issues become so deeply rooted in our daily lives that they seem inescapable. Therefore acknowledging pain makes us better at recognizing healing. In fact, if we cannot acknowledge our pain in the first place, the chances of healing are greatly diminished. Embracing reality when bad things happen means we have hope for the future. This is true for small, personal troubles and larger, communal troubles as well. If we acknowledge that the person in the office next to ours is a drain on our energy, we can be careful about how much effort we put into that relationship. If we see that someone is drinking too much or family members chronically fail to communicate with love and respect, we can reach out for help. We can work to set healthier personal boundaries. On a larger scale, if we acknowledge that people are discriminated against because of class, race, or gender, we can speak up or act when the opportunity presents itself.

I am still learning to turn to God with my deepest pain. The ghosts of classism, racism, and sexism that still haunt the world, the loss and loneliness I experienced as a child, the pain I caused others—these are just a few examples of my personal encounters with destruction.

After I finally acknowledged the destruction present in my life, I discovered my fear of dreaming about restoration. I no longer avoid the bad feelings when they occur, and I make a daily effort to dream a new dream, to sing a new song, to imagine how God's healing and restoration can occur.

This passage in Isaiah points us to the joy and abundance that come in the restoration that follows destruction. We often forfeit the promise of joy and comfort depicted here by becoming trapped in our grief about what has happened to us or what we have done wrong. We become mired down in all the ways our lives have gone wrong because of our own doing or otherwise. In these times of grief, we may choose to remember joy, restoration, and a way out of no way. After acknowledging our own pain, we must dare to dream of God's restorative mercy, hope, and joy to get us through the dark times.

My daughter has a friend at her elementary school who runs to hide when something bad happens to her—if she trips on the playground or if someone says an unkind word. My daughter is troubled by this and has said, "Why won't she let me be nice to her when she feels bad?" I suspect this is a very common response to pain: we recoil from comfort out of fear—fear of admitting what has happened, fear that it might happen again, and fear that it cannot be made right. This fearful reaction is not just common in little girls; I have seen it play out with soldiers returning from war, public figures, and with myself.

These verses from Isaiah encourage us to embrace troubling times and times of destruction. This passage reminds us that restoration follows destruction. Joy will return for us as it did for Jerusalem.

REFLECTION QUESTIONS

1. When have you hidden from a destructive habit, an inevitable life change, or a toxic relationship you could not bear to face?

2. How have you sought comfort in God?

3. How do you take your worst behaviors and darkest problems to God? How do you sense God's embrace in these times?

4. What are your childhood memories of being nurtured and cared for such as the ones depicted in Isaiah 66:10-12? If your childhood was lacking in nurturing love, how can you provide feelings of comfort and love for yourself?

WRITING EXERCISES

1. The images from this passage—the life-giving sustenance of mother's milk, the physical joy of a child being held by an adoring parent—are potent. Make a list of other images that evoke the same depth of joy, nurturing, and happiness.

2. Verses 10 and 11 have four lines. Verse 12 has five. Using this basic structure, write a poem calling for someone

you love to celebrate your renewal. Or write a poem to a loved one celebrating his or her renewal.

3. The book of Isaiah tells us of the Messiah who will come to bring salvation. As Christians, we believe this is Jesus Christ, one person of the Triune God. Some believers can name the day and time when Christ appeared in their life and became their Savior. Some Christians grew up with a faith that was simply part and parcel of their lives. Write your story of salvation or the one you hope will come to you.

4. Name the various areas of life you have experienced or could experience some kind of devastation, loss, or disappointment. Now choose one and write in detail what restoration and renewal would entail.

Seventy Sent Out
Luke 10:1-11

Jesus sent out seventy followers to spread the word and offer healing. Some cite this passage as the beginning of the mission of the Christian church. Here we see one of the ways Christianity, which started as a Jewish sect in first-century Palestine, departs from its Jewish roots. The hallmark of this departure is that Christians become missional, focusing on evangelism. Judaism has a rich history of welcoming strangers, but I do not see the same kind of focus on sharing the message and making converts that I see in Christianity. This push to make converts and spread the Word has resulted in some life-giving outreach as well as some of the bloodiest of "holy" wars.

We can practice evangelism through different methods or not at all. Our personal experiences with evangelism inform how we feel about it. We may have happy memories of being ministered to, or we may recall with anger feelings of intimidation and manipulation. Reflecting on this scripture passage reminds me of all the different methods of evangelism and mission work I have seen, most of them rather unlike the account of Jesus sending out the seventy.

When I was a child, a family traveled through our town regularly to preach, offer salvation, and threaten hell. The family members were loud and boisterous, a husband and wife with their grown son. The images they conjured in their preaching were colorful and shocking. They relished describing details of human depravity and mocking "polite" people for the look of discomfort on their faces. When I saw them coming to town, I felt conflicting waves of curiosity and fear. I did not want to be the object of their preaching and mockery, but I very much wanted to see what they would do next. One of their lines was "Jesus sent us out two by two, and we got three! Father, Son, and Holy Ghost!" The father would say *Father*, the son would say *Son*, and the mother would shout *Holy Ghost*.

I encountered other types of evangelism by attending church services from time to time with friends, usually small country churches that frequently held revivals with guest preachers. At their churches, I heard fearsome sermons followed by prolonged altar calls asking people to come forward and repent of their sins, accept Christ, and be healed of their diseases. During these altar calls, music played. Sometimes someone would sing an emotional song about sins and regrets. Often the preacher would walk back and forth as if he were pondering the fate of the flock, occasionally crying out for repentance. Once I encountered a Pentecostal church service called a *crusade*. There was music and laughter and weeping. This was back when live bands were unheard of in church services, at least in small towns. Let me just say, the Pentecostals I knew could rock the house. They were known as "holy rollers" for several reasons as far as I could tell. I found it both exciting and a little frightening. My home church was many times the size of their small church, and yet I had never encountered the amount of sound that came from that small gathering. And no one in my congregation ever got slain in the Spirit.

Then there was the church I grew up in and loved as a child. I cannot remember anything about us that brings to mind the sending out of the seventy. I would ask my mother about the words the pastors used, and she would make me look them up in the big dictionary at home saying, "It will build your vocabulary." My church had a choir and a youth group, a couple of trips a year for the elderly and youth, Sunday school classes for all ages, and a fine, large building. In many ways we were probably guilty of the criticism that we were just a social organization, but I hate to think of where or to whom I might have turned had I not attended that church. I do not remember once tending to the sick or feeding the poor. I do remember that the church felt like a safe place for me when other parts of my life did not feel so stable. Perhaps I was the church's mission? Does that look anything like Jesus' commission to the seventy?

And then there's my current tribe, sometimes called "the frozen chosen." At the governing level, the Presbyterian church appears to put a great deal of time and money into serving others and reaching out to the sick and hungry of the world. But on the individual church level, the Presbyterian church resembles many mainline denominational churches that maintain expensive buildings primarily for the use of their own members. I have been involved with local Presbyterian churches that are very active in the feeding and healing of the community, but just as many exist primarily for members drawn to commune with each other on Sundays.

My encounters with the fiercer kinds of evangelism made a big impression on my childhood and early youth. I sometimes found myself wondering if my congregation was really

Christian enough, as I heard it once referred to as one of those "lukewarm" churches. I worried and wondered about my parents and about myself, how we might fare if this version of eternity turned out to be true. The passion and certitude exhibited by people who claimed to know who would and would not make it to heaven felt overwhelming. I found myself craving this certitude at times, and other times repulsed by its narrow intensity and judgmental attitude.

Truthfully, all traditions I have encountered left me with something to ponder. The more comfortable I grew with my own faith journey, the more I could view others' with interest rather than fear. Even charismatic but unethical leaders demonstrate that our deep, human need for belonging can make us vulnerable to abuse.

God is too big to pin down into one, tidy interpretation, one building, or one way of being. And our brokenness and imperfections constantly poke through, making trouble, even in the best-intentioned churches and missions. Our journeys are long, beautiful, and perilous. Keeping in mind the various ways people have responded to Christ's commendation to the seventy helps me to stay interested in how I have been sent out into the world. How am I to heal, how am I to proclaim the gospel? I ask myself again and again, *What is a straightforward way to evangelize, a way that simply offers help and acknowledges God's kingdom come?*

REFLECTION QUESTIONS

1. What do you believe about healing? What healing have you participated in or received?

2. What do you think about those who have gone out in the name of Christ but abuse the people who follow them? What experience do you have with such people?

3. How do you offer the healing, restorative good news of the gospel? What would you do if you were turned away?

4. Who has evangelized to you? How was the message delivered? How did you receive it? What form of healing was offered? What images of God's kingdom were used?

SUGGESTED EXERCISES

1. Write out the specific instructions given to the seventy and the scene as if it happened in the current day. What would be the equivalent of shaking the dirt from your sandals? Think about your current context. Do you live in a city, suburb, or rural area? How would the seventy reach people? How would they travel?

2. Imagine you are a member of one of the pairs sent by Jesus. Write about a typical day. What types of people do you meet? What living conditions do you encounter? How are you able to extend Jesus' message of liberation and restoration?

3. Some say Christ had the disciples stay in the "same house" in a community throughout their sojourns in order to avoid the human temptation to move from house to house for better housing, food, and drink. Write about this temptation. Is there a present-day correlation to this?

4. Have you experienced being a lamb in the midst of wolves? If so, write about that experience. Was God in that experience with you? If you sustained some sort of harm from this experience, did you find healing and restoration? If so, how? If not, what would restoration and healing look like were you to receive it now?

2

Water for the Thirsty

S ometimes we need cool water to quench our physical thirst. Sometimes we need the refreshing water of God's grace to quench our spiritual and emotional thirsts—our thirst for acceptance; acknowledgment and love; direction, purpose, or meaning. Sometimes we need spiritual water to counteract a situation that has deadened our heart and mind. Receiving healing spiritual water when we are in need can be as life-giving as drinking a cool cup of water when we are thirsty and tired. Sometimes when we have been in a difficult situation for a long time, we get tired of waiting for that water of life. Sometimes we close our hearts against healing and deliverance for fear our hope will be disappointed. We may lash out against the very people trying to help us. The scripture passages in this chapter explore some of the ways we thirst and some of the ways God sends us cool, clear water.

Rainbow Eggs
John 4:5-26

This story of Jesus and the Samaritan woman is like a moment in a movie when a gang member meets a person from a rival gang. There they are on the outskirts of the city, in the heat of the day. She doesn't understand why he is in her territory. Out of the blue, he asks her for water. Something is up; something is different. What is about to happen?

Jews and Samaritans disagree over claims about God. The Jews of first-century Palestine believe they practice the original religion of Abraham, Isaac, and Jacob. The Samaritans believe they are the keepers of the true religion. Each group holds deeply ingrained negative thoughts and feelings about the other. In this passage from John, the main difference noted is the disagreement about how and where to worship God.

Just imagine how tense this woman must be when she sees someone from a hated group approaching her. Is she questioning his perception of her—does he see her as unclean and wrong in her beliefs? Consider her surprise at the end of the encounter when she walks away blessed exactly as she is and commissioned to be a disciple to her people. Jesus recognizes her worth. He sees her fit to carry his message; her words mean something. This must feel like living water indeed.

✑

My father's two most common parenting phrases were, "You should be seen and not heard," and "Put your hands in your pockets, and keep your mouth shut." These pieces of advice helped me navigate times when I found myself in adult company or someone's home filled with expensive items. But as a way of life, following his advice seemed impossibly restrictive. I remember feeling that there was no way for me not to be a pest, an annoyance, and a source of embarrassment to my father, who seemed larger than life, heroic, and all-important.

I see now that my father had his own tensions and troubles that prevented him from finding delight in parenting me. As a chattering, curious, irrepressible child, I only added to his stress. I tried to keep myself quiet, but that was like trying to settle a soda bottle that had been shaken and opened. When I spoke, my thoughts bubbling over, his angry words humiliated me, put me in my place as quickly as possible, and effectively silenced me. While Dad got relief from my chatter, I began to believe that I was, at the core of my being, an annoyance. This belief took its toll on me over time.

Not surprisingly, I recall with clarity and gratitude the time an adult asked me a question and listened with interest and appreciation to what I had to say. One of the ladies at church asked me if I had dyed Easter eggs. I told her I had tried to make a rainbow egg by mixing the colors together. I said, "I thought it would make a rainbow, but the colors got too mixed, and it made more of a mud swamp color." When she laughed, I braced myself for criticism, thinking this was yet another time I had been an annoyance to an adult. Instead she responded, "That is such a wonderful description!" And then she repeated my words back to me. "'A mud-swamp color!' What a way with words!"

Her complimentary observation was living water to me. Through this simple exchange, I realized I could be delightful, that I had good ideas to share, and that others would want to share their ideas with me as well. Decades later, I still cherish this memory and replay it when I need a source of hope and joy. I held onto that moment and locked it away in my heart so I could take it out when needed—whenever I got thirsty—to remember that I matter. This encounter gave me the fresh perspective I needed for a different view of myself and eventually for a different view of my father as a person with his own struggles and feelings.

✍

How much more shocking and life-giving must Jesus' words be for the Samaritan woman? Jesus tells her every detail of her life, unclean as it might be. He chooses her to be a messenger of his gospel of liberation and hope. Jesus dissolves the toxic barriers between them as Jew and Samaritan and allows them to interact with love and respect. The kind of living water he brings to this woman is strong enough to send her back to her community to proclaim she has met the one, the Messiah, the Christ. Any time we share the good news of God's love with someone who is feeling inconsequential or unappreciated, we offer living water.

REFLECTION QUESTIONS

1. What do you know of belonging to a class or race that is hated by others? What life experiences sent you the message that you were less than? Which people, if any, were you encouraged to view as less than based on class, race, or history?

2. How does God work in your life to provide wholeness in the face of your sense of alienation or emptiness? When you catch yourself looking elsewhere for acceptance, what helps you receive the acceptance offered by Christ?

3. What does the term *living water* mean to you?

SUGGESTED EXERCISES

1. Write the thoughts of the Samaritan woman as she sees Jesus approach the well and as they talk. What thirst does she live with day in and day out?

2. Write from the perspective of one of the men this woman had married previously. What is it like to see her

coming into town with Jesus' message of good news?
What is her attitude toward you? What is your response
to her story of the living water?

3. Write about a time you felt you were not seen or heard.
Now write about a time you were seen and heard; or, if
you have not yet experienced this, write about what it
would feel like to be seen and heard for who you are.

4. Jesus is able to turn water into wine. He is able to feed
thousands with just a few loaves and fishes. What does
it mean that he asks the Samaritan woman to give him
water? Why does he do this? What effect do you think
it had on her?

Water from a Rock
Exodus 17:1-7

As a child in church, I heard the Bible read in somber, respectful,
serious, fiery, and fearsome tones. Never light or with humor. The
first time I remember laughing during the reading of the Bible,
the preacher was reenacting these verses from Exodus. My husband and I were visiting a church out of town. The preacher more
or less did a stand-up routine depicting the people Moses brought
out of slavery only to find themselves wandering in the desert.
The preacher did a great job of showing what a horrible disappointment it must have been. Like some cruel joke, the Israelites
were given an amazing promise of liberation and were then led
around in the desert. He made great jokes about the "Back to
Egypt Committee" and all the whining and complaining that
must have gone on after the parting of the Red Sea—"So God can
part the waters but can't find the way to the Promised Land?"

The preacher retold the story from various points of
view. He recited a monologue about what God must have been

thinking—hadn't God delivered the Israelites from slavery, led them safely away from Pharaoh, fed and protected them? They have the nerve to complain about being thirsty?

The preacher played the role of Moses as well. Poor Moses. He never really wanted the job anyway. He tried to get out of it because of his stuttering problem. Still, after Moses' best attempts to escape this work, he becomes the leader of a raggedy bunch of liberated slaves meandering around in the middle of nowhere, not impressed with a miracle when they see one. They have no faith, and they are thirsty. According to Moses, they plan on stoning him if he doesn't provide water—and fast.

I can still see the pastor "putting on" as he played Moses, complaining about the Israelites who would rather go back to slavery than wander around in the desert waiting for God. They bemoaned the sand in their shoes from crossing the parted sea. Then finally, Moses struck the rock and water poured forth to quench the thirst of the people. And they grumbled yet again, saying, "Oh great, all this water, and we have no cups!"

I could not believe what I was hearing from this pastor. I laughed so hard my sides hurt. It felt great! I encountered this church at a time when I felt fairly removed from the people and stories of the Old Testament. I had always loved the stories for their plots and twists, but I did not feel connected to these books of the Bible.

This pastor's humorous take on Moses made me feel connected to the Israelites. I could see myself in their story. How many times had I reached a goal or been delivered from some hardship only to feel dissatisfied, wishing I had done better, gotten more recognition, or achieved a higher level? I remember the way my mother used to give me a certain amount of money to spend for my birthday and inevitably—no matter the amount she set aside—I would always want to spend a little more for just one extra item.

I can see how the Israelites feel their lots in life have gone from bad to worse—now they are wandering around in the desert trusting that God will send them enough food and water for every day. Even if slavery lies behind them, how is the unknown much better?

The Israelites exhibit not just a lack of gratitude but the state of humans in general. We have an enormous capacity to complain and forget. Even when we have lived prayerfully—fed by the Word and sheltered by love—difficult times can make us fearful and forgetful.

When God made a covenant with the Israelites, God did not say that they would never encounter hardship, pain, or seasons of waiting. God's covenant instead promises love, belonging, and the hope that they could live into this loving relationship with joy and humility.

I cannot remember what theological argument the pastor was making that day when he put on such a show. But I do remember how I felt. Having a good laugh at the humanity I share with the ancient Israelites brought me into the story. Their story became my story too. It gave me space to renew my covenant with God, to acknowledge my own fear that God might let me die of thirst, and to release that fear by recognizing the many ways in which life-giving water flows from God and sustains me.

REFLECTION QUESTIONS

1. When have you laughed in church? What experiences link humor and studying the Bible?

2. When have you been delivered out of a dreadful situation but then found yourself facing other difficulties?

3. What experiences would you consider miracles of deliverance?

4. When have you lived through a period of wandering, a time in which you felt truly lost?

SUGGESTED EXERCISES

1. Imagine how Moses felt when his own people were getting ready to stone him because of their thirst. Write a paragraph or more from his point of view.

2. Imagine how the Israelites felt—no longer enslaved but now wandering in the desert. Write from the perspective of a small child observing his parents and his community as they seek to solve the problems and face the realities of the desert.

3. Write about a time you experienced distress and could see no way to get relief. How did you get through that time? What happened? Can you relate to the feeling of deliverance that the Israelites might have had when seeing the water flow from a rock in the desert?

4. What does the Israelites' release from slavery and entry into the hardships of the desert say about God? Ask God all the questions this might raise in your mind.

When Tempted to Harden Our Hearts

Psalm 95

The first few years of marriage were really difficult for me. I had grown accustomed to being the center of my universe. I had my own money that I spent on whatever I wanted, saving and spending as I saw fit. I had my own home that I opened and closed to others as suited my moods and needs. My space was quiet when I needed peace and full of friends and music when I needed community. My time was my own. I only did what I wanted and went where I wanted to go. When I married Stan, I gained three teen-aged children and learned a whole new way of being. I became a player in four other universes instead of being the center of my own.

The kids took to me, and I took to them too. Still, they were navigating those difficult adolescent years and now had a stepmother. I was working out what it meant to be a wife and stepmother after I had spent all my life as a free spirit. Stan was working out what it meant to be married again and how to create a family with me while his relationships with his children shifted and changed.

Not long into the marriage, my new family encountered conflict. All our hopes, fears, bad habits, and eccentricities got tangled up with one another. After a year of this, I found myself cranky all the time. I felt tired, stressed, and unsure of how to go about the various tasks of my new life. I had no measurement for success. The bottom line was this: I had met the man who was a friend of my soul, my true love, and the difficulties of life were hardening my heart to the life we could build together. We had been so happy to find each other. Why had the celebration stopped after the wedding reception? Where had our happiness gone? What happened to our dreams? We needed to get through those wilderness years.

Going into the second and third years, I was depressed, and I cried at the slightest complication. I scrutinized Stan constantly. I felt like a failure as a stepmother. I lost my compassion and joy. I was not finding my way through the wilderness, or so I thought.

One day I had lunch with a friend who confided in me that she had been jealous of my marriage and family. "Why?" I asked. "We are a mess."

"Yes, I know," she replied, "but both you and Stan are trying for the same thing—to be better people for each other and for the kids. Even if you never get it right, you have that. You are really trying to be who you are and belong to each other."

What a reality check. It was true. Stan never faked who he was with me, and he never asked me to fake who I was. Our lives did get better—and then sometimes worse. We faced many challenges, muddling along, experiencing the good, the bad, and the ugly. Knowing we belong to something greater than ourselves can be easy to overlook when life gets hard and does not turn out as we hoped and dreamed. However, simply belonging is worth celebrating.

Stan and the kids taught me how to love, and that love has everything to do with being willing to persevere even when all you see is wilderness. Experiencing the acceptance of my husband and stepchildren taught me about the meaning of love—I didn't have to be perfect or always measure up to others' expectations. Love is a lot about accepting each other and circumstances as they are and doing the best we can with what is even if we are aiming for something better. I experienced healing by celebrating each day—its joys and disappointments—while not letting my heart harden as I waited for a miracle, for water to pour forth from the rock.

This basic acceptance, but on an even deeper level, is what God's covenant seems to be about: we belong to one another. This covenant is not a magic genie's lamp. It is not the promise of an easy life. It is the promise that we are always loved, we always belong, and we will be cherished in good times and in bad. From that place of acceptance, wisdom sometimes reveals itself. Healing can begin. Meaning takes root. To live as if we are loved and accepted invites purpose and meaning to fill the empty places in our lives.

The psalmist calls for us to celebrate God and cautions us to not harden our hearts as the Israelites did at Meribah and

Massah. We are to praise and rejoice because God is the creator of all things and we belong to God. Let this acceptance flow like water from the rock to all God's creation.

REFLECTION QUESTIONS

1. The psalmist writes from God's perspective saying, "For forty years I loathed that generation" (v. 10). How can living with a hardened heart feel like being abandoned by God?

2. Several passages in the Bible depict God as punishing and vindictive. How do you understand these passages if you believe in a loving, merciful God? How do you understand them today in a way that promotes compassion, love, and healing?

3. Psalm 95 calls for celebration. What ways of celebrating would you include if you were the author?

4. The psalmist calls God the "rock of our salvation" (v. 1) and "a great King above all gods" (v. 3). What metaphors would you use to describe God? What ways would you call people to celebrate God?

SUGGESTED EXERCISES

1. Write your own eleven-line psalm calling your people (your family, your church, your study group) or yourself to celebrate. Refer to a time when you (or the group of people to whom you write) turned away from God while waiting on water to pour from the rock. Use your psalm as a reminder not to hold a hardened heart as the people did at Meribah and Massah. (See Exodus 17:1-7.)

2. Write a letter from God to the writer of Psalm 95. Have God respond to the lines in which the psalmist imagines what God might say (vv. 10-11).

3. Write an eleven-line psalm about waiting in acceptance, with an open heart, even as you travel through the wilderness without enough water to sustain you.

4. Write an invitation to a celebration of God. What would that party be like? Where would it be held? Who would be invited? What would be served? What music would be played? What stories of miracles would you share?

3

Nothing Wasted

S ometimes we look back on our lives and see how we made choices that wasted time, love, and relationships. We may wonder what good could ever come of our mistakes, what redemption could emerge from our sorrows. Feeling as though we have wasted a part of our lives can leave us stuck in guilt and shame. However, God may have other plans for our misadventures and errors in judgment. God's kingdom come may not look like what we expect. The selections for this chapter explore the ways we wrestle with our past, how God can make use of the entirety of our lives (not just the moments we feel good about), and the nature of abundance in God.

Crossing the River to Wrestle
Genesis 32:22-32

The first funeral I ever officiated was for Beverly, the mother of my friend Alexia. Through Alexia I got to hear a lot of stories about Beverly. She was the daughter of an upper-middle-class

Southern family, a golden child who had her doting father wrapped around her finger, who enjoyed extravagant birthday parties, ponies for Christmas gifts, vacations in the summer, a swimming pool, and trips to New York for buying clothes. Beverly had been an accomplished horse rider—winning many blue ribbons in competition—a musician, and someone generally admired by men and women alike. Beverly was clearly a charmed and charming girl and woman, charismatic, funny, and beautiful.

Taking responsibility for the funeral was daunting, however, not only because Alexia means so much to me but also because her relationship with her mother had been fraught with tension. Alexia also told me stories of her mother's struggles, bad decisions, heartache, and a wild party spirit that eventually turned into grinding addiction. She was fabulous and flawed, flamboyant and feisty. She loved Alexia fiercely and yet had acted and spoken in ways that clearly showed she was not in control of her own life. For Beverly, cultivating healthy, intimate relationships was not her greatest skill.

Thinking about Beverly and how to eulogize her—to celebrate her joys and acknowledge her struggles in life—I was reminded of Jacob as he travels to meet his brother, Esau, for the first time since Jacob stole his birthright. Jacob leaves his family and animals on the opposite side of the Jabbok River. He spends all night wrestling an angel in a furious match. Jacob finally says to the angel, "I will not let you go, unless you bless me" (v. 26), and he gets his blessing. But the angel wounds him on the hip, and from then on, Jacob limps.

I love this story because it gives us courage when we are wrestling angels—or demons—and reminds us that we must demand a blessing. But also it hints at this wisdom: When we are wrestling, we are separated from everyone we love. They are across the river, and we must wrestle alone, without friends or family.

Beverly was often separated from those who loved her, particularly near the end. Some of the separation was her own doing, but at times others separated from her. Either way, a wrestling was taking place. As Beverly wrestled alone, the loved ones she left behind were wrestling for their blessings as well. And so it is with all of us. At some point in our lives, we will be utterly alone and forced to wrestle for and claim our blessings. I think Jacob's story encourages us to extend grace to ourselves and others, knowing this kind of wrestling requires hard work.

Jacob's wrestling begins and ends in the course of one night, though it is the beginning of a lifetime of struggling—and walking with a limp. From talking to Beverly's family and friends, I saw that she too wrestled for a lifetime. She asked multiple times for a blessing, crossing the river every time.

Beverly had been baptized at a Baptist church downtown. She grew up in a home where scripture was read as a matter of course and, like a good Baptist, she could quote chapter and verse at the drop of a hat. Going through Beverly's things, Alexia found notebooks where Beverly wrote out scripture and added her commentary, what she thought the verses meant and how they addressed her life. She also asked questions, pages and pages of questions, about how life worked, where God was, what she was supposed to do in her life. Many of us wrestle with questions about our purpose or value. We wrestle for the hope that our wrongs can be redeemed and used for good.

Beverly struggled with God. Though she affirmed her faith that God had created her and had a plan for her, she admitted that she didn't know all the answers, that she was confused at times about the decisions she made and the circumstances in which she found herself—some too sad to repeat and some too good to be true. She often said that the first thing she would do when she saw God was get some answers about why life is the way it is.

Jacob builds his adult life on the stolen blessing of his brother, Esau. Even this, God does not waste. Rather, God brings Jacob to a place and time to wrangle with this part of his past. This gives me hope that the many times Beverly wrestled for her blessing were not wasted. Clearly, she struggled with her faith and her path in life. The events of life that unfold as we act and are acted upon in this world can be painful and miraculous, oppressing and liberating.

In God, we find that our lives are not wasted. We can embrace the opportunity to be apart and wrestle with things we have done or what has been done to us. Wrestling for our blessing, we find a meaningful way forward in life.

REFLECTION QUESTIONS

1. Do you know someone like Jacob or Beverly, someone who struggles with decisions made early in life, someone who has to fight for his or her blessing?

2. Imagine how frightened Jacob must have felt to be going to see his brother for the first time after he had stolen his blessing and birthright. What went through his mind? What do his wives and children know about his fears and worries?

3. What are the wives and children left on the banks of the river thinking as Jacob goes across to wrestle? Are they hoping for a changed Jacob? Has he been hard to get along with lately? Do they know what's going on?

4. Think about this angel with whom Jacob wrestles. Is this an angel or God? Does it make a difference? Why does the angel wound Jacob?

SUGGESTED EXERCISES

1. What gives Jacob the nerve to demand a blessing? Write about what he might have been thinking. What qualities would you have to summon within yourself to demand a blessing?

2. Write about a time you wrestled with a difficult situation until you won your blessing. Ask God to give you a name to represent your struggle, demand, and victory. Write about this name and what it means to you.

3. Some say this "angel" with whom Jacob wrestled was actually God. Seeing the face of God was supposed to be too much for a human to survive. Write about this idea and why or how Jacob survived.

4. Write in detail about some part of your life that feels wasted, whether by your own actions or the actions of others that impinged on your life. If you have already wrestled with this part of your life and been blessed, write about that. Prepare a safe way to burn the paper upon which you have written to signify that you give this part of your life to God to be remade for God's purposes alone.

God Will Use It All

Isaiah 55:1-13

This passage in Isaiah conveys the incredible joy felt at the end of the Babylonian Exile. After everything had been taken away, the Israelites are going to be restored. This passage reminds me that I cannot comprehend the mind and ways of God. Sometimes I find this a great comfort; other times I just want what I want when I want it—with or without God. Often I simply cannot see how God is going to make a cypress grow where thorns have been. I cannot foresee how God will use rain and sun and wind to make my life blossom as a myrtle would take root and grow. Sometimes life seems too random to ever come together and make sense.

This sense of randomness weighed on me as I made the decision to leave one career and return to school for training in another. I left my profession as a college literature teacher to start years of study that might (or might not) lead to a new career. With jobs harder and harder to come by at the university level, this decision felt like closing a door rather than opening another. I would also be older than most of the other students at divinity school. At one point many older men and women were going back to school to pursue study and work in ministry, but that was when the economy had been "good." When I quit my university job, everyone was just holding on to what they had. After prayer and discernment, my husband and I came to the conclusion that it was the right path for me and our family even though we did not know how things would work out in the future. My closest friends and family offered unconditional support, eager to hear about each new semester.

I also encountered people who openly opposed the idea of a woman taking on theological training and ministry, some who found my quest too unreasonable to discuss. Others' snarky comments were difficult to interpret. When speaking with persons about my plans, I never knew whether to expect support or criticism and disapproval.

Perhaps most daunting of all, my path back to the church and into divinity school had been rather roundabout. I assumed my peers would be primarily younger men and women from distinct church backgrounds and straightforward paths leading from high school to private religious colleges to graduate work in theology. Instead, I learned and grew with peers and professors of all ages. Those years of study launched me into new work that made use of every aspect of my past. I could not have known any of this the summer before my first year of study, though, and so it was a godsend to meet a doctor named Roger who had completed a Master of Divinity some years before. He inspired me to hope—before I had proof—that God could pull together the various strands of my life and make a cohesive whole.

Roger had grown up thinking he was going to be a forest ranger but studied pre-med to satisfy his parents. Though he did well in school, he only took his medical school qualifying exams after leading ocean kayaking tours and working as a chef. Eventually he became a doctor. With these varied experiences in his past, he could speak to people's difficulties finding an exercise and dietary plan that worked for their lives and limitations. Later on, he realized what a large part religion played in his patients' lives and decided to learn more by pursuing his own M.Div. in theology and religion.

While my history was not as impressive as Roger's, I noticed the commonalities in our circuitous paths. We talked a long time about the various roads we had traveled, people we had met, mistakes we had made, and wisdom we had earned. One thing he said, though, made an enormous impact on me: "You'll see. God will use it all. God doesn't waste anything. I see it in the way the body works, and I see it in people's lives." His words kept me going through hours of study and long nights of self-doubt.

Now, as I find a way to write with people to heal old wounds and open up new ways of relating to God and the Bible, I see it: Nothing is wasted. When I meet people from different Christian denominations or different religions I once explored, I see it: Nothing is wasted. When I talk to young women who feel lost, who cannot imagine how precious they are and what purpose their lives have, I see it: Nothing is wasted.

Through my service as a hospital and hospice chaplain, I found that many of my most painful life experiences helped me relate to patients. Some of the most obscure side roads of my life journey provided ways of connecting to people who needed to know they could trust me for genuine pastoral care in the face of their suffering and not just a bunch of pretty words. I am still discovering that God does not waste anything. I can trust and enjoy the process of meaningful interactions revealing themselves, of sense coming out of nonsense, of nothing being wasted.

We are invited to turn to God—to turn ourselves over to God—and to see what happens. The rain will fall, and it will go into the earth. The earth will produce bounty. Trees will grow where there were thorns, myrtle where there had been briars. We may feel lost at times. We may find ourselves in exile. Still we can trust God; nothing is wasted.

REFLECTION QUESTIONS

1. The Bible is full of reminders that God's thoughts are above those of mortals. Life in God can be too mysterious for comprehension. How do you experience this mystery in your life?

2. What qualities can we attribute to a God who will "abundantly pardon," as mentioned at the beginning of the Isaiah passage?

3. What kind of God brings forth a cypress from thorns and a myrtle where there once were briers?

4. What periods of your life seemed useless? How has your perspective on these times changed?

Suggested Exercises

1. Write about a time in your life you felt was a waste. How did God use this time for some other purpose?

2. The writer of Isaiah uses the poetic images of a cypress growing where there were thorns and the myrtle growing where there once were briers, mountains singing, and trees clapping. Write a list of your own images that exemplify the good that can come from a time of waste or exile.

3. Verses 6 and 7 speak of returning to the Lord. Write about actions that cause you to turn away from God, and then write what God's pardon does to bring you back. Write a letter to God about this offer of abundant pardons.

Nothing Wasted, but Plenty Left Over
Matthew 14:3-21

In verses 13-21, Jesus feeds the multitudes. In the passage just before it, Herod also feeds people (vv. 3-12). The two stories are interesting to view side by side. The earlier passage tells the story of murderous rage and greed in a setting of—and perhaps exacerbated by—opulent abundance. The second passage tells the story of abundance that comes out of pursuing God even with the simplest of means.

We can imagine that the tables set for Herod's birthday are filled with the finest food of the season, musicians play for the occasion, and the wealthier citizens of Judea, as well as a few representatives of Rome, are gathered, wearing fine clothes and jewels and prepared to have a good time. I doubt the guests wonder if there will be enough to eat or drink.

On the night of his party, Herod's niece dances for those in attendance. Both literature and myth have made the dance infamous. The Bible says that Herod is so enthralled by her performance that he promises her anything she wants. On her mother's behalf, she asks for the head of John the Baptist. The Bible's silence has sparked much theory about exactly what the dance entailed and about the nature of Herod's enthrallment to his niece. Even without the erotic and possibly incestuous overtones, the story is disturbing. Political intrigue, money, and power reign in this story.

In comparison to the lavish party and the gruesome beheading of John the Baptist, we have Jesus who withdraws to a quiet place after receiving the news of John's death. People from town find out Jesus' location, and they follow him. They show up in droves to hear him speak, to be healed, to learn, or maybe just to be near him. After hours, it is too late for people to return home—the children are tired, the adults do not want to drag their families around in the dark. Everyone is hungry.

When Jesus tells the disciples to feed the people, they think of what has to be bought and prepared to feed such a crowd. The disciples are practical, knowing they have only five loaves of bread and two fish, but Jesus sends them out into the crowd anyway. In the end, everyone is fed. There are even leftovers. Healing, community, and simple but miraculous abundance are the hallmarks of this story.

The message Jesus delivers to his world through his healing, teaching, and feeding undercuts the power and importance of Herod. Jesus teaches from the Mosaic Law that people belong to God and God belongs to the people. We can express this spiritual truth in all our relationships, including those with family, friends, money, strangers, animals, and work. The way we live should reflect our beloved belonging to God. This message seems dangerous to rulers like Herod who are owned by worldly powers. This message must have been very difficult for people who expected a Messiah to become a king on a throne.

To matter in the Roman Empire, a ruler requires an appetite for greed, power, and success at any cost. To participate in the kingdom of heaven, we must be open to healing, to miracles, to the gathering of God's people for the purpose of restoration. Herod illustrates the ruin created by blind ambition, betrayal, the use of sex and manipulation, and the low regard for human life. Jesus shows us healing and teaches us we are inherently full of value as God's children. With just a few loaves, Jesus feeds multitudes—nothing wasted, but plenty left over. The hallmarks of God's abundance are building relationships, healing, caring, and showing respect.

REFLECTION QUESTIONS

1. What does the kingdom of heaven look like to you? Where do you see the kingdom of heaven in the feeding of the five thousand? Where do you see it in your life?

2. Think about the difference between the two gatherings—Herod's party and Jesus' five thousand. Which one would you want to attend? Why?

3. What parts of your life are most like the account of Jesus feeding the crowd? What experiences looked more like Herod's party?

4. Are you surprised to read the account of Herod's niece's dance? How is Herod's response to his niece different from Jesus' response to the Samaritan woman at the well? What do they have in common?

Suggested Exercises

1. Think about the disciples' reason for sending the people away. Write about this experience from the perspective of a disciple.

2. For whom or what would you travel miles to see? A concert? A preacher? A celebrated teacher? A friend? A family member? Have you ever run into difficulty feeding yourself or others while on a trip? Write about your experience.

3. Think about the sick people who traveled to see Jesus and find healing. Write about your trip and your healing as if you are one of the five thousand. What did you witness and how did it make you feel when you saw loaves of bread that multiplied as they were shared?

4. Write about an experience of abundance in which nothing was wasted. Then write about an experience of abundance that bred greed and misery. What caused the difference between the two?

4

When God Is with Us

In the passages shared in this chapter, we see God offering deliverance to broken people. Often we find it difficult to look past our own brokenness to the gracious gifts God offers us. From our limited perspective we strain to imagine the deliverance God is offering us. How would we feel if we had been at the eye of the storm the last days of Jesus' ministry? What would we do if Jesus suddenly appeared to us, just as we had lost all hope? How would we respond to God if we were told we had been picked to carry out God's will?

It's Not What You're Doing, Martha—It's How You're Doing It
Luke 10:38-42

What did Mary understand that Martha did not?

Once I studied this passage with a group of women. We talked about how to be Martha—work hard, clean the house, put food on the table, take care of others. These are the activities Jesus seems to tell everyone else in the Gospels to do when he asks people to feed and heal others, build God's kingdom, offer hospitality. We believed that the story compares Mary's personality to Martha's—one a work-focused person and the other a sit-at-the-feet-of-Jesus person. We agreed that Jesus contrasts striving to work and do (Martha) with loving and adoring him (Mary).

Then one of my friends said, "I just wish I could be more like you, Jane. You don't let housework get in the way of soaking up God's Word!"

Knowing this friend's love for me, I believe she spoke from her heart. But knowing myself, I understand that I just hate housework. Sure, I'd rather read the Gospel of Luke—and every commentary written about Luke—than mop my floors. Yes, my house is a mess. But this is not due to a depth of spiritual acumen. I still feel more like anxious Martha than peaceful Mary. And to me, that is Martha's main issue. The problem is not with what she does—Jesus mandates that we care for others, feed the community, show hospitality, and serve. The problem is that Martha is distracted. Mary finds peace at Jesus' feet; she is not a worrier, and her peace cannot be taken away. I have a hard time believing that Jesus thinks Martha is doing something wrong. Martha has lost her peaceful center. She is adrift in worry and anxiety. Jesus isn't pointing out that she is doing too much housework but that she is worried and anxious.

Why is Martha anxious? Why is she troubled?

Martha is an intelligent, hardworking woman. She may be well aware of Jesus' current situation—in Luke 10:25-37, an expert in the law questions Jesus' interpretation of scripture. What ensues is not a friendly conversation. The Jewish authorities aligned with the power of the Roman Empire distrust Jesus. Martha understands that Jesus' situation may get worse before it gets better. And Jesus' situation *does* get worse. Jesus will find himself in the middle of other disagreements with Rome and the Jewish authorities. Ultimately Jesus will face betrayal, prolonged torture, a public crucifixion. His disciples will scatter. Jesus brings good news to the poor and the oppressed, and there are those who desperately need his word of hope. Martha, however, knows his message isn't going over well with everyone.

Jesus comes to proclaim that we are God's beloved children, that what the government says we are doesn't matter, that what the powers and principalities want us to believe doesn't matter, that our brokenness doesn't matter. We are God's beloved children, and this is what matters. We are commended to live as if we know how deeply we are loved. Anxiety and worry are not our inheritance.

When we find our center, our calm heart in Christ, this is the peace that cannot be taken away by the world. Even if we are more like Martha and do not feel the security of God's love, we can hold onto the hope of this reality. Breath by breath we ask God's love to become our experience. Prayer by prayer we hold ourselves open to the possibility that we can live and feel and experience life as beloved children of God.

Mary sits in dignity at Jesus' feet. Mary shows us what it looks like to have a spirit not weighed down by anxiety. Mary shows us what it looks like to believe Jesus' good news, even when the storm clouds gather. Even though Jesus is in the room, Martha's anxiety prevents her from being *with* God. Mary embraces her Lord and puts everything aside that could cause her distress. God is with both Martha and Mary, but only Mary is with God. God is in Mary's untroubled spirit.

REFLECTION QUESTIONS

1. How does worry consume your thoughts? What do your friends or family members say about your worrying?

2. Many people interpret this passage as a comparison of
   two personality types—Martha as the worker bee and
   Mary as the contemplative. What are your thoughts?

3. What would life feel like if you decided not to worry
   about things you cannot change? What would you
   do with the time and energy you used to spend on
   worrying?

SUGGESTED EXERCISES

1. As a worrier myself, I imagine that Martha might feel
   slighted and shamed by Jesus' scolding. Write how she
   might have responded to defend her worry.

2. Imagine how Martha would feel to be free of her worry
   if Jesus released her from the anxiety about what
   was to come. Imagine how her work preparations for
   guests would have been different. Write from Martha's
   perspective about how she will act in the future.

3. Rewrite the story as if it took place in the present year.
   Try this several ways, using different cultural and
   socioeconomic settings.

You Mean Me?

Exodus 3:1–4:21

Five times Moses talks back to God in an attempt to prove he is
not the man for the job. This extended passage is worth reading
again and again. Try it out in different voices, imagining that
Moses might have been afraid, or lazy, or simply lacking in
faith. He might even have been sly, trying to wriggle out of the

job because he could clearly see how dangerous it was going to be, hoping God would choose someone else.

We have the freedom to ignore God's call. I often wonder if Moses isn't weighing the pros and cons of being called by God in this passage, perhaps stalling God through argument. He may be thinking about how much easier his life would be if he had never stopped to take a second look at that burning bush. Though Moses is slow of speech, he possesses some sort of temper or inner strength that caused him to strike out against an Egyptian and kill him for abusing one of his Hebrew brothers. (See Exodus 2:11-12.) Moses is hardly a shrinking violet. He resists, refutes, and argues with God.

Consider the burning bush. At the center of this fiery bush that does not burn is God with a plan to deliver the Israelites. God appears to Moses because the cries of the Israelites are great. God will deliver the oppressed. When Jesus comes, he preaches about liberating the oppressed as well. Throughout time, God is concerned with the oppressed and calls people to work for liberation.

Even today, we see that oppression still exists. Communities in North America are oppressed; entire countries around the globe live in states of oppression. Oppression is not just about poverty and prejudice; in some of the most exclusive communities in the world, physical, mental, emotional and spiritual oppression exist. I know many middle-class Americans who feel oppressed, living paycheck to paycheck to keep a house in a neighborhood with a safe school.

We cannot all be called to minister to others in all these cases of oppression, but God is calling each of us. In some way or another, God wants to use us to deliver not only others but also ourselves. From early childhood there may be clues to God's calling on our lives. As long as I can remember I loved to visit shut-ins. I had a list of elderly men and women that I went to see on Saturdays and holidays. I loved books and animals and praying alone in my mother's garden. Then I became a teenager. Girls in my town wanted to be cheerleaders and beauty pageant winners. I distinctly remember choosing between my books and elder visits and my new life as a part of the social scene. I often think of this time in my life as the moment when I, like Moses, stalled and tried to haggle with God about my identity.

Moses kills an Egyptian and escapes the city with his father-in-law's sheep. No sooner does he drive the sheep across the desert to Sinai than he comes across a burning bush. What makes him stop to consider the bush? Why doesn't he run the other way? These questions draw us nearer to God, and we slowly step closer and closer as Moses must have approached that fiery bush. And when we hear God call our name just as God calls Moses by name, we may then have a few questions for ourselves. *Why am I resisting God? Why am I refuting God's plan? Why do I feel like I'm not up to the task? How can I find the courage to answer?*

REFLECTION QUESTIONS

1. Reread the passage. Put yourself in Moses' position—a man of two nations, a murderer, a husband and son-in-law, a man whose true people are hated. Walk in his shoes as he crosses over to Sinai, sees the burning bush, and begins his extraordinary conversation with God.

2. Think about your earliest experience of showing compassion for someone or some group you perceived as oppressed.

3. Near the end of the passage, God tells Moses that Abraham will help him. Who have been the helpers in your life?

4. What kind of oppression do you see in your immediate community? How are you called to be part of its liberation? How are you oppressed in ways God may be calling you to address?

Suggested Exercises

1. Rewrite the scene of the burning bush as it might look in the twenty-first century.

2. Write a report on Moses' attitude as if you were a school counselor, he were a student, and God were his teacher. What would you tell Moses' parents about his relationship to authority, and what might you recommend to his parents?

3. Imagine a conversation between God and yourself. God is telling you about a man named Moses who does not seem to understand what he is called to do or who is calling him to do it.

4. Write a letter to God discussing all the times you have resisted God's call on your life. Be honest about why you resisted and what kind of behaviors came about in your life as a result of resisting. Or if you did not resist—or eventually responded—write about the resulting life experiences.

Anything to Eat?
John 21:1-14

When I was in college I had a dog named Isabel. She was my constant companion and therefore the companion of my closest friends as well. For about two years, I dated a wonderful man named Jack. We spent as much time together as we could, and the three of us—Jack, Isabel, and I—would often go on long walks, spend afternoons in the park, or study at a local café where dogs were allowed.

When Jack and I broke up, neither of us really understood what was happening. We knew our relationship had changed, or rather, that we had changed and our relationship had not been able to do the same. I remember the night we talked about it—we both cried. Neither of us knew what was ahead or why we had grown apart. We still cared for each other.

I am sorry to say that I did not handle the breakup very gracefully. Jack tried to be a friend, and I could not seem to do the same. I hid. I immersed myself in new friends and new activities. The stronger the emotions of grief and loss became, the busier I kept myself, the more parties I attended, the more new people, places, and experiences I sought.

One day, I drove to a nearby market for groceries with Isabel. The weather was beautiful, and I rolled my windows down. As I pulled into a parking place and gathered my purse, Isabel suddenly barked and leapt from the car through the open window. She had spotted Jack walking along the sidewalk. She wiggled and wagged and barked and jumped. Every cell of her body was expressing how she felt, how much she had missed Jack, how delighted she was to see him again. I waved awkwardly from the car until he took up her leash and handed it to me through the window and went on his way.

∽

Growing up listening to Bible stories, I heard this passage in John many times—so many times, in fact, that it did not really mean all that much to me. Not until many years later—when I was in my forties—did Peter's exuberance become real to me. I took on the exercise of rewriting the story in my own words, imagining the words the disciples and Jesus might have spoken.

The memory of seeing Isabel leap from the car to greet Jack flashed in my mind, and I finally understood the unabashed joy I suspect Peter felt.

As a woman in her forties, I understood myself better than I had in college. I began to learn about parts of myself that had remained hidden from me—the things that truly brought me happiness, the various fears that knocked me off balance, the fear of abandonment, as well as the urgent need to see more of the world, to feel confident in my own perspectives, to pursue my hopes and dreams. Finally I could understand the humility and simplicity required to let my feelings—particularly joy—show freely, despite my fears of criticism and judgment.

Isabel was able to recognize the one she loved and the one who loved her. Isn't this what our relationship with Christ calls us to do? Without shame or guilt, without wondering if we really are part of God's plan, we may leap out into the water and paddle furiously toward our beloved Christ. Or we may not. We may hide our faces, lost in confusion and hesitation.

Christ had not simply gone away for a few days. He had been brutally crucified. All that he had spoken of and promised seemed to have ended. The disciples didn't understand what Christ's good news was supposed to look like during the forty days after the crucifixion. The miracle of Jesus was real to his followers but very much a mystery in terms of what would happen next.

We still live in a time of mystery. Even in the United States, where we often have our faith handed to us by generations of tradition, we each face living into the mystery of the Christ who has come but who has not yet come again. We each need new and renewed ways of living into this time of not knowing.

How do we live now? How do we embrace Christ now? How do we leap into the water and swim toward love? How do we accept ourselves when we hang back and can't find the courage to run in the direction of the one we love? What happens when Christ disappears from our lives for a time? How do we respond when we find him pitching camp on the shore, building a fire, asking if we have had anything to eat? What happens when we say, "No, we have not had a bite to eat! We're coming to eat with you—the one we know, the one we love."

REFLECTION QUESTIONS

1. When have you "fished all night" and watched the sun rise over your empty nets? Ponder that hopeless feeling of working hard at something and not succeeding.

2. When have you given up all hope only to find that everything worked itself out? Consider the role of blame and guilt in loss of hope as well as the relief and joy that comes when things turn out not to be as bad as expected.

3. How receptive are you to joy once your plans are disrupted? How do you respond when the beloved comes your way?

4. Think of a time you shared a meal with friends you had not seen in a long time. How did the love shared between you affect the taste and experience of the food?

SUGGESTED EXERCISES

1. Rewrite this passage from the perspective of Christ who knows the hearts and minds of each of the disciples.

2. Why do you think the disciples fished all night with no success only to be told by Jesus to cast their nets to the right in order to catch a boatload of fish?

3. What did it mean for the disciples to go fishing after the crucifixion? To what activity do you turn when you feel distant from God? Does it take you closer to God

or further away? What conversation might the disciples have had when they decided to go fishing?

4. Jesus calls to the disciples and asks, "Children, you have no fish, have you?" (v. 5). When Jesus calls your attention to your own hunger, how does he do this? Does he direct you to cast your nets differently? How so?

5

Loving and Being Loved

I do not know whether I am more surprised to find Christians who believe God excludes certain people from God's love or to find Christians who have open minds about how God regards the entire world. Open-mindedness was not highly valued in the community of churches I attended as a child. One of the reasons I left the church was this lack of open-mindedness. To this day, I remain baffled by some people's obsession with excluding others—those from foreign lands who practice religions other than Christianity or those who simply appear to be different—from God's love. I hope the scripture passages in this chapter inspire us to consider our relationships with others as extensions of our loving relationships with God.

A Friend in Need

Ruth 1:1-18

Naomi, her husband, and their two sons live in Moab because of a famine in their native land of Judah. While in this foreign country, the sons marry Moabite women. When her husband

and both her sons die, Naomi is left alone with her daughters-in-law, Orpah and Ruth.

Naomi's story is one of loss after loss after loss. She finds herself stripped of every opportunity a woman of this time could hope to possess. The loss of her husband means the loss of security, safety, and identity in her community. The only image that could evoke more fragility and vulnerability would be that of an abandoned or orphaned child.

Orpah does what seems to make the most sense. When Naomi releases her to return to her own people and find a husband, she leaves. Yet Ruth refuses. The author of Ruth offers no explanation for her steadfastness other than the words of attachment Ruth speaks. Perhaps she feels protective of Naomi. As another single female, however, Ruth can provide very little for Naomi. Even after Naomi points out that she has no other sons to offer to Ruth in Levirate marriage—a brother of the deceased man marries his widow and cares for her—Ruth remains by her side.

Naomi and Ruth return to Naomi's home in Judah and together they create a life through mutual affection and loyalty. Not only do the women find a way to survive, but they also find a way to thrive. Love, respect, and creative effort come out of Ruth and Naomi's alliance. New life is the result.

When I think of the loss in this story, I am reminded of my mother's death. The grief I experienced after losing her made me feel isolated and alone. Though my other family members grieved as well, I could not connect with them. I wonder if Naomi feels this loneliness and grief when she tells her daughters-in-law to return to Moab.

A friend came to my aid in my time of loneliness, just as Ruth helps Naomi. My ability to provide for myself was not at stake, but my ability to reenter the world was. My friend called out to me when I got lost in missing my mother. My friend did not intrude upon my grief but merely stood close enough to draw me out of my grief, much as Ruth draws out Naomi.

The loss of my mother will always be part of my story, but I did not have to stay in grief and loneliness forever. I came out of the haze of loss and reentered a life that holds many stories yet to unfold. Thank goodness for friends like Ruth.

REFLECTION QUESTIONS

1. Have you ever lived in a country, region, or neighborhood where you felt like a foreigner? Describe how that experience felt to you, or try to imagine what it would feel like.

2. The Mosaic Law provided for the ethical treatment of foreigners who resided among Israelites. What does this mean to us today?

3. Loss can make you feel like a foreigner. Have you experienced such loss—the loss of a loved one, financial loss, or emotional loss? How does the love of others help you heal from loss and find life again? How can you be the source of such love for others?

SUGGESTED EXERCISES

1. Write from the perspective of Orpah when she hears that Ruth and Naomi have gone to Judah to seek shelter with Ruth's family. What does Orpah think of this God to whom Naomi has returned and whom Ruth will soon meet? Does Orpah miss Naomi and Ruth?

2. What did Ruth see in Naomi that made her willing to go against custom and return to Judah? How did Naomi's religious beliefs affect how she treats Ruth? Use your imagination and allow these people to speak to you about their world and experiences.

3. Ruth and Naomi's story is one of the few in the Bible with women as main and supporting characters. Ruth, a Moabite, furthers the lineage that will produce King David and Jesus. While God's plan is referred to, God is not an overtly active part of this narrative. What does this story tell us about God?

4. Write about a friendship that has meant a lot to you. Write about when you met, how you came to know each other, and what important events you have shared.

5. In Ruth's time, women face the same concern: maintaining access to resources through alliances with men and through childbearing. Today, the concerns of women vary greatly from nation to nation and even community to community. Yet some women still live in a world much like Ruth's. What are the concerns of the women in your world? Write a letter to God about the status of women where you live—either in your neighborhood, your state, your country, or beyond. Express your concerns and voice your hopes and dreams for women.

God!

Luke 11:1-4

As a hospice and hospital chaplain, one of the most common issues I see people dealing with is the inability to forgive. One of the primary blockages to peace and well-being seems to be the inability to forgive ourselves or others—often both. I do not know if this lack of forgiveness blocks us from God's love or if blocking out God's love is what prevents us from forgiving, but we often feel cut off from God when we deny the act of forgiveness.

The Lord's Prayer addresses our need to forgive and be forgiven. I have known and recited this prayer for as long as I can remember. When I was very young, I feared many things: school, adults, the future, and the unknown. My mother taught me this prayer and encouraged me to use it as a way to focus my mind and feel safe and close to God. Sometimes the prayer kept my mind occupied and brought relief; sometimes it did not. I still worry and feel anxious from time to time, and I use this prayer as a way of pulling my attention away from worry or fear to instead focus on God. An experience I had some years ago gave me a new insight into the prayer and brought a fresh energy to the way I pray it.

When I was a new wife and stepmother, life seemed so difficult. I worried a great deal. As I wrote in an earlier chapter, I experienced this worry for a long a time. I was either mad and judgmental—designing strategies to fix everyone—or sad and lethargic—wanting to give up. Even after I was able to embrace the goodness of our lives together and appreciate our way of caring for one another, I found myself lost in regrets. I could not shake the lingering feeling of disappointment caused by others and myself. My family was important to me; gratitude for them would often overcome me. But sometimes I fell under the shadow of doubt, believing we had not lived up to some ideal in my head. A gloomy feeling of inadequacy had accompanied me since my youth, and as an adult, I continued to experience it.

One day I went walking in a local city park. Over the course of the one-mile trail through a wooded area, I began to feel critical, sad feelings. Why couldn't I shake the feeling of regret? When would I stop replaying scenes of selfishness and small-heartedness? When would I cease holding my imperfections against myself and against those I loved? Finally I had grown tired of the negative thoughts playing in my head.

Emerging from the woods, I headed toward the walking path by the lake. At one end of the lake, some branches had fallen into the water. Thousands of luminous bubbles covered the submerged limbs. The bubbles were frog spawn. The gelatinous eggs were shimmering underwater as the late afternoon sun shone over the surface. They clung to the branches like blooming flowers.

Mesmerized, I bent down to look at the eggs. A woman I had not noticed coming toward me suddenly appeared at my side. She crouched down next to me, covered head to toe in a *hijab*, her tan face and intense, kohl-rimmed eyes watching me questioningly. I pointed at the little blooms of eggs in the water, and we both gazed at them.

She smiled at me, stood up, raised her hands in the air, and reached toward the sun saying, "Allah! Allah!" She motioned to me to get up, nodded her head, and did it again, as if she wanted me to join in. She looked at me puzzled when I didn't do anything. "Gud, Gud" she said to me, flinging her hand at me like it was my turn.

"God!" I said.

"Yes!" she said smiling and turned to walk away.

Honestly, it was such a surreal moment I sometimes wonder if it really happened, though I know it did. Its effect on me was both immediate and lasting. Tears came into my eyes, as if I had seen something surprising and beautiful, like a rainbow or fireworks. The way she immediately turned her awe for the pretty clusters of eggs into praise for God made me feel as though I was walking on holy ground, that the world was holy ground, that even I was holy ground. This feeling of God's all-encompassing holiness had escaped me for quite some time, and I didn't want to let it go. When the old thoughts began to press upon me again as I made my way across the park to my car, I could feel the way they diminished this sense of the holy. I did not want that to happen. Recalling the beauty of the moment I had just experienced pushed the negative thoughts away.

In comparison to the quiet holiness of nature and the woman's immediate praise of the divine, I could see how the negative feelings I had been harboring dimmed my light and shut me off from feeling God's presence. I learned how strong my negative thinking could be and how vulnerable I felt when trying to overcome it. Praising God, sensing the holy, experiencing joy—these actions helped me find the courage to ask forgiveness for my own harsh thoughts and behaviors to free me from my negative thinking, to heal me of the abiding sense of unworthiness, to allow rejoicing in the family I love. Encountering God's holiness did something for me that I could not do on my own.

No wonder the Lord's Prayer begins with God—"hallowed be your name." We turn to God, who offers love beyond our understanding. Then we can turn to ourselves and to others in forgiveness, acceptance, and love. God's forgiveness does not excuse bad behavior, but it releases us from the conviction that we must fix the past or other people. God's forgiveness allows us to open ourselves to the possibility of joy. God, us, them. All on hallowed ground.

REFLECTION QUESTIONS

1. Is there a prayer or practice from another religion that has helped you be a better Christian?

2. What is your relationship to the Lord's Prayer? Does it feel vital and alive or does it feel like a stiff, empty ritual?

3. How do other religions fit in with your beliefs about God? Is this question a no-brainer or does it feel too big

to answer? Do you have set ideas about other religions, or are you open to exploring new thoughts and ideas?

SUGGESTED EXERCISES

1. Rewrite the Lord's Prayer in language that fits your life today.

2. In what ways is God's name hallowed? If God is the creator of all, how does holiness show up in creation? Write about an experience in nature and if you felt God's presence there.

3. When you recite the Lord's Prayer, you might say, "Forgive us our trespasses, as we forgive those who trespass against us." Write about what this means to you. Look up other translations of this line. Write your own translation of this line.

4. What does "on earth as it is in heaven" mean to you? In a letter to God, ask for insight into God's will "on earth as it is in heaven."

One and the Same

Mark 12:28-34

The commandment to love our neighbors as ourselves has always struck me because it presupposes that we love ourselves. I have heard that in some cultures the idea of hating ourselves does not exist. I don't know if this is true, but from what I can see, the American culture practices self-hatred with ease.

If our national rates of violent crime are not proof enough, just watch live television for a few hours, and you will find all the proof you need that Americans struggle with self-hatred.

We are told that if we could just make more money, get skinnier and healthier, convince more people to like us, buy more stuff, look more attractive, seem smarter, funnier, and sexier then we could feel good about ourselves. We are just one product, promotion, or service away from being our perfect selves.

As a woman, I am bombarded by promises of "As Seen on TV" products, and they can still stir within me a hopeful feeling that I am just about to discover the secret to my greatest happiness, deepest self-love, and best hairdo ever.

To love our neighbors as we love ourselves points us inward first, but what if we struggle to love ourselves in a real way? I have never met a person who doesn't struggle with a deep loneliness, some bottomless emptiness, or a darkness that is scarier than anyone wants to admit. I've seen a few extraordinary people deal skillfully and honestly with the hollow places inside themselves. These people seem prepared to love their neighbors as themselves.

Most of us, though, harbor something inside of us that we have a hard time looking at, much less loving. How then will we find the inner strength and security to love our neighbors? By neighbors, the Bible does not just mean those who live next door to us but those in the next nation and on the next continent as well.

Because we find it difficult to name this inner emptiness and because we put so much time and energy into running from it, we often project our fears and disappointments onto the outside world. These projections make it even harder to love people who now bear our perceived imperfections and flaws. We project our fears on others, and they may project those fears right back at us.

Often we try to simplify how we see others by reducing them to either "the good guys" or "the bad guys." As a chaplain at a military hospital, I found that some veterans of foreign wars struggle with reconciling the job they performed as soldiers with the knowledge that those "others" aren't so distant or unfamiliar or different. While it may be enlightening to think others are just like us, it is not always easy to know how to live that out, particularly when being just like us means they struggle with sin the same way we do.

Maybe loving others is the way we learn to love ourselves, just as loving ourselves is the basis of our love for others. The love my family shows me eventually emboldens me to soften my criticisms of myself and causes me to revisit some of the decisions I made about my own unworthiness. Caring for patients as a chaplain humbles me as those I care for offer love and appreciation in deep, meaningful ways. When I offer my time to listen to others' laments, the expression of love and gratitude that flows out of them is palpable.

Whenever I face anxiety about a group of "others," I try to recall this passage about loving our neighbors. I may find it difficult to apply Jesus' words to my life, yet Jesus says this love brings us into the kingdom of God. Getting to know neighbors—whether next-door or across national borders—is not easy. Getting along as humans and living with mutual respect means acknowledging that humans of all cultures exhibit qualities that make some easier to love than others. Yet it is worth it once we embrace ways to share, give, communicate, and live harmoniously together.

REFLECTION QUESTIONS

1. How do you love God with all your heart, soul, mind, and strength?

2. How do you show love and respect for yourself, and how does this affect the way you treat others?

3. In what ways do you not love yourself? What things about yourself make you most uncomfortable? How do guilt and shame block healthy self-love?

4. What do you find hardest to love about others? Does loving others seem frightening or unsafe? Obsession, addiction, and control are often mistaken for love. What would loving others in a healthy way that mirrors God's love look like?

SUGGESTED EXERCISES

1. Jesus is summing up many laws into an essential value. If scribes were to ask you about your faith, what would you say? Write this response.

2. Jesus says that love—of God, neighbor, and self—is at the core of the law. Write about times you experienced love of God, neighbor, and self.

3. At this time in Jesus' ministry, persons are questioning his teachings. Write about a time you were questioned about your beliefs. Did you feel love for or from the people who questioned you?

4. The essence of God's law—love—runs contrary to how the competitive, consumption-oriented world works. Think about the activities you turn to when you feel low, for example shopping, eating, drinking, and gossiping. Write about the allure of the world and compare that to what God's love does for you. Write about ways you can turn to love when you feel bad about yourself.

6

Sins Like Scarlet, Clean as Snow

L iving in a broken world, we all experience what the Bible calls *sin*. When we are not sinning against others or ourselves, we remain part of a world fraught with systemic evils. I've struggled to make peace with the word *sin*. Pastors who preached about sin during my youth used the term as a way of controlling and scaring people. In my own religious circles today, I do not hear this interpretation of the word *sin*. The hellfire and brimstone take on sin must still be taught somewhere, though, because I meet plenty of frightened people who have been convinced that when they die their sins will engulf them in burning flames.

My husband and I often talk about sin as "missing the mark," since that is the definition of the Greek word for sin, *hamartia*. This understanding of sin leads not to scary conversations about missing the mark but to discussions of what "making the mark" might look and feel like. The Gospels explain that making the mark would be to live as if we know we are loved, and as if we know others are loved as well. This is not so very different from what Moses and Jesus tell us is at the heart of the law—to love God with our entire beings and to love our neighbors as ourselves. Falling short of this ideal, as we all do, results in sin.

A Story with Good Bones
John 3:1-19

The Greek word in verse 3 of this passage, *anagannao*, which is so popularly translated as "born again," is more literally translated "born from above" or "born from on high." The "born again" Christian might more accurately be identified as "born from above." This more literal translation points to the fact that not only is coming to life in Christ a rebirth, but also that this birth comes from God and not from our human nature.

Nicodemus is a Pharisee. During his ministry, Jesus does not get along with the chief priests and Pharisees. Perhaps Nicodemus seeks Jesus at night so that others will not see him visiting a troublemaker. Nonetheless, Nicodemus comes to talk to Jesus about the miracles and powers he has been exhibiting and to discuss Jesus' relationship to God. Nicodemus tells Jesus that what Jesus is doing looks not like the work of a human but the work of God. Jesus does not spend a great deal of time answering Nicodemus's question about his own reality in God. Rather, he tells Nicodemus how all people can enter the kingdom of God: They must be born from above.

I have often heard people talk about being born again as if it took place in a single moment when their sins were washed clean and life was never the same again. But I feel that a better understanding is that God makes and remakes us over time. Being born from above is different from our physical birth in many ways, and being born from above does not occur only once. Rather, being born from above is a process that happens over a lifetime. Birth from above is God's continual action of grace in our daily lives.

When we rely on God to be spiritually present in our physical lives we are being born from above. Our human abilities and personal striving cannot save us, but God can. If asked when they were saved, some people in my church have been known to answer, "About two thousand years ago." An emphasis on God's saving work is typical of Reformed theology. We are not responsible for—or able to accomplish—salvation ourselves.

I can point to several occasions that had a great impact on me, moments or events in which God broke through my humanness and offered me new life. I think of these times as episodes of grace. I cannot explain them and I cannot control them or make them happen. These moments come from God.

Is it possible that a new birth is already beginning in Nicodemus? Is this birth what brings him to Jesus in the night? It is clear from what he says that he has been watching Jesus, listening to his teachings, observing his healing powers, taking note of what people say about him and how they behave after their encounters with him. Perhaps Nicodemus comes to see Jesus at night because he wants to be alone with him to speak at length and at ease. Perhaps he comes to see Jesus at night because he does not want to compete with the crowds of people who gather around him in the day. Most of all, perhaps Nicodemus pays a personal call to Jesus hoping he will share knowledge and bring light to his questions. Nicodemus seeks a new life.

We read later in John's Gospel that Nicodemus builds a relationship with Jesus. In John 7, Nicodemus even defends Jesus, despite the influence of his peers, the chief priests, and the Pharisees. Nicodemus asks them to take a step back, to look into their investigation of Jesus a little more closely before

making a judgment against him. Furthermore, after the crucifixion when Jesus' body is taken from the cross, Nicodemus
brings about seventy-five pounds of myrrh and aloes in order
to prepare Jesus' body according to custom.

When I consider these passages, I like to imagine myself
as Nicodemus. I allow my imagination to fill in the gaps of the
story from the basic details we are given in scripture. This story
has what I call "good bones." The Bible tells us of Nicodemus's
actions, but we are left to wonder what goes on in the mind and
heart of the main character. Nicodemus's thoughts and feelings
can vary greatly depending on how we fill in the blanks as we
read, depending on our perspective as we read, and depending
on the details that stand out to us at any given time. A friend
calls this reimagining of a story "dreaming the story." She finds
a comfy place to rest, closes her eyes, and actively allows the
images of the story to unfold in her mind's eye as dictated by
her imagination. The Living Word really comes to life when we
play it out in multiple scenarios and through the eyes of different characters over the course of our lives.

REFLECTION QUESTIONS

1. Have you had a "born again" or "born from above"
   moment? Which translation speaks more to your
   experience?

2. Even after being "born again," life contains both ups
   and downs. How do you understand this reality?

3. What is the relationship between your human nature
   and that which is born in you from above? How do
   these two coexist? Jesus understands this kind of dual
   nature since he was from above but came into the world
   fully human. How can you reconcile the differences
   between your two natures?

SUGGESTED EXERCISES

1. "Dream the story" of Nicodemus. Pick one of the characters, or another character you invent to observe the story, and imagine the story in as much detail as possible. Write down the dream or the basic impression left behind by the dream.

2. Write a poem about your own Nicodemus-like experience (or that of someone else you have observed) using these words and expressions: born from above, womb, water and spirit, wind blows, heaven, not condemned, darkness, light, and teacher.

3. Imagine seeking out Jesus at night, being received by him, sitting at a table with a candle or lamp burning between you, and conversing with him on entering God's kingdom. Write out this scene as if you experienced it. Use as much detail as possible to describe Jesus, yourself, and your surroundings.

4. Write about a time you stood up for someone else against your better judgment and without really knowing why you chose to defend him or her.

Jesus' Posture of Forgiveness
John 8:1-11

At this point in my life, perhaps no scripture passage means more to me than this one in John. Though it is a story I have long known, I came to love it a few years ago. Every aspect of the story—the accusers so desperate to trap Jesus, the woman used in such a charade, and Jesus writing in the sand—fires up my imagination in a way no other passage does. This is the passage my professor assigned for reflection when I first experienced writing back to the Bible. He read the verses to our small gathering of seminarians and local pastors. Then he invited us to write with, to write into, and to inhabit this story as our own. This is the first passage that truly spoke to me in the way I imagined the Bible spoke to others.

When I was in seminary, I took a "What is your theology?" quiz in one of my classes. I discovered that my experience of God was more "once born" than "born again." At no time in my life can I not remember sensing and loving God. Yet I still encountered some hard years when I felt confused and far away from God, years in which I felt separated from God and my humanity in a painfully acute way.

This woman brought before Jesus to be judged reminded me of those difficult years. As I wrote, I became that woman—the shame and guilt she feels were the same shame and guilt I had felt about everything from poor performance on a fourth grade spelling test to my own unworthiness. This exercise brought forth uncomfortable feelings, but I experienced Jesus' presence in the room—or more accurately on the page—with me. Jesus stoops on the ground and writes in the earth with his own hand. Jesus—the incarnate Word—draws me in with his silence and bent posture. And when he speaks, he does not even address my transgressions and the shame I feel. He says that if anyone there has not sinned, he may cast the first stone. Jesus knows what the leaders want to hear. They want Jesus to recite the Mosaic Law decreeing that an adulterer must be stoned to death. They want him to either violate the Law of Moses or to violate his message of radical love and forgiveness. Jesus does neither.

Writing with this passage was exhilarating. There with my peers, sitting in silence, I heard scripture speak to me clearly about my life. I found my own story there in the Gospel of John. I immediately knew I was not alone; Jesus was with me.

I knew Jesus saw me and understood me in a deeply compassionate, forgiving, and creative way. Jesus was inviting me to experience myself in this way as well—to believe this of myself, of life, of God. Jesus offered wholeness, even as I stood ridiculously exposed in all my brokenness.

Then my professor asked us to share what we had written. Siting at the table with me were men and women I greatly respected, people I wanted to befriend, possibly impress, or at least not repulse. How was I going to share what was happening with me without revealing my own shame and guilt? How was I going to admit the experience I was having without first coming clean about my difficult and very slow to grow relationship with the Bible?

I don't remember what I said, but I do remember how close I felt to my classmates by the end of the day. Let me put it this way: I was not the only one having an intensely personal, life-giving experience that left me feeling painfully vulnerable. Years later, I am still friends with the men and women who were in that room. Some I see more often than others, but that day lives within each of us. We allowed our brokenness to be revealed and experienced the love of Christ in unique ways. Then we shared those feelings with one another.

My experience in that classroom reminded me of a story my cousin told me when I was twelve years old about a church she attended. She told me that her mother went before the entire congregation and confessed something she had done. The episode my cousin described struck fear in my heart. I could not imagine standing in front of a church full of people and talking about the things my cousin said her mother had to confess. I could not even believe my cousin knew about it. To this day I am not entirely keen on this practice. On the other hand, I have found myself wondering if perhaps my cousin's mother felt the same way I did when she owned her actions, her shame, and her guilt. Perhaps in doing so, she saw Christ, stooped over,

pressing his finger into the carpet and leaving behind imper-
manent letters and words. Perhaps her confession allowed the
congregation to feel what those of us gathered at the writing
table felt that day—none of us was free of sin, and therefore we
could befriend one another. We did not have to wear masks to
hide our hurts and shame. Jesus set us free from our sins and
our shortcomings through his posture of forgiveness.

REFLECTION QUESTIONS

1. Have you ever been entrapped by someone? Or have
   you ever tried to catch someone in an act for which you
   hoped to see him or her judged? Think about times you
   failed to let an argument die when you could easily have
   let it go.

2. We do not know what Jesus wrote in the sand. Why do
   you think this detail is not given?

3. When have you judged other people for something you
   have also done or judged others by standards you do not
   uphold yourself?

4. What shame or guilt have you been carrying?

SUGGESTED EXERCISES

1. Write what you think Jesus wrote in the sand.

2. If the woman were to write a letter to Jesus, what would
   it say?

3. Write from the perspective of someone watching this
   drama unfold.

4. Rewrite the story in a contemporary setting with
   familiar languages and characters.

A Clean Heart, O God

Psalm 51

I have come to understand that everyone I meet—even the most confident person, even the sweetest soul—carries some grief or sadness. Every time I walk into a hospital room, that grief or sadness is there. At every retreat, in every prayer group, in every consultation, it is there. People don't always want to talk about it. That is normal. If we only thought of our grief, we would get stuck in depression and hopelessness. The ability to put our feelings aside can be a great gift. On the other hand, there are times to let our sadness out, to experience the shame we feel over the past, the hurt we carry, the grudges we harbor, the tears that never seem to end. Whether our burdens are laden with our own sins or the sins of others, writing about them and envisioning life without them can be part of our healing process.

After I began using writing in my work as a chaplain, an older patient spoke with me about the Psalms. This patient talked about how much he loved God and how many things he had done wrong in his life—the things he had messed up, sins he had committed, and hurt he had caused others. This patient told me how much he loved reading the Psalms and thinking about King David. He said he related to David's love for God, anger for his enemies, sorrow over his sins, longing for wholeness, and fear when God seemed far away. David experienced it all; this patient had too.

David wrote Psalm 51 after Nathan came to confront him about having taken Bathsheba. Not only did David take the wife of Uriah, one of his soldiers, but also he put Bathsheba's husband in the line of fire in order to have him killed. This psalm is one of the most famous of the seven regarded as the

Penitential Psalms, calling out to God to repair the personal and social disorder brought about by sin.

This psalm is divided into three parts. In the first part (vv. 1-10), the psalmist asks for deliverance from sin. He is not only concerned about the sinful action; he speaks of the emotional state that brought it about, the physical aspects of the sin and its consequences, and even the social disruption wrought by the sin. Sin is so often not just a single act but an entanglement in rotten feelings and toxic relationships.

In the second part of the psalm (vv. 11-19), the psalmist is asking for something even greater than the forgiveness of sins and the blotting out of transgression. He asks to be made near to God again. Nearness to God brings deep joy and restores a sense of well-being and wholeness. Clarity and the abundance needed to share ourselves with others in community and in happy, healthy interpersonal relationships accompany this joy. This nearness allows us to share with others what it is like to be free of sin and embrace our belovedness in God.

In the final section of the psalm (vv. 20-21), the psalmist desires the restoration of God's whole kingdom. He envisions a renewed relationship with God for all people. The psalm describes a time when human worship and praise please God.

Even if we have not committed the kind of sin David did, this psalm can be applied to any sorrow we carry or to the brokenness afflicting creation. Often, if we are the ones who have been sinned against, we carry the burden of that sin, unable to get free of the bad feelings associated with having been wronged. The Bible shows us again and again that God's love is meant to be felt and lived on a daily basis. We have to find ways for our belief and faith to enter into our lives and lift the burdens of pain, stress, anxiety, and guilt. One way to do this could be writing our own psalms, through which we can interact with scripture and with God.

The patient I worked with found both relief and joy in this writing practice, eventually finding a way to talk to his family about parts of his life he had not been able to share before. As the psalm implies, forgiveness is not for us alone but a miracle that can bring a sense of joy and wholeness back to our whole lives and our world.

REFLECTION QUESTIONS

1. What are some emotional, social, and physical aspects of sin?

2. How comfortable are you with the word *sin* and all it implies? Does the phrase "missing the mark" make more sense than the word *sin*? Perhaps sin is simply that state of separation from God, the state into which we are born and live unless we find methods of connecting and surrendering to God's love.

3. Consider making some time to read the books that include David's story: 1 and 2 Samuel, 1 Kings, and 1 Chronicles. How would David's story play out in contemporary times?

SUGGESTED EXERCISES

1. Write your own psalm of repentance. Use the three-part structure of Psalm 51 as a guide. First ask for deliverance from all the aspects of sin you can imagine. Then ask for nearness to God and describe what that joy and clarity would be like. Close by depicting a world free of sin and separation from God.

2. Make a list of all the sins you think you have committed. Then make a list of all the sins that have been committed against you or in which you were somehow caught.

3. Make lists of all that you learned about human nature and life through the experiences you have had, even the ones sinful in nature. Think or write about the ways you might share your hard-won wisdom with others who are vulnerable.

4. Write a letter as if you are King David. Perhaps you are writing a letter to the twenty-first century about God. Perhaps it is a letter to yourself about a certain event.

Leader's Guide

This guide offers several ways to use *One Day I Wrote Back*, including a few tips on how to lead small groups and methods for practicing the writing exercises alone.

Note for the Leader

The group leader needs to be someone who embraces questions and is not alarmed when people express doubt or uncertainty. The leader will set the tone for the group, encouraging people to write in whatever form they choose or are able. The writing done for these groups is not to be critiqued for its literary or compositional value.

You might choose to set these rules with your group:

1. When it is time to share writing or thoughts, any participant may pass. A participant may remain silent during group discussion, or if sharing proceeds by going around the group, those who do not wish to share may say, "I pass."

2. Each participant may speak to or about his or her own experience and feelings but not to or about the experiences or feelings of others in the group. This is not a time to offer advice.

3. Comments on others' writing will consist primarily of gratitude. For example, the leader might say, "Thank you for sharing" after a participant speaks.

4. What is shared in the group needs to stay in the group. Confidentiality is important. Consider writing a covenant in which members agree not to repeat what is said in the group to those outside the group.

Small-Group Guide

The following meeting format will be repeated six times over the course of six weeks as the group progresses through the chapters. Each member of the group should have a copy of *One Day I Wrote Back*, a Bible, and something in which to write (by hand or in digital format). Everyone should know the time and place to meet as well as the contact information of everyone in the group. The Leader will bring a white candle or a tea light to serve as the Christ candle.

Dedicate the first meeting to defining the group covenant and writing with the first meditation from Chapter 1. Setting the tone and rules of the group—perhaps including aforementioned examples—may take twenty to thirty minutes. Schedule two hours for the first meeting. Thereafter, the leader may adjust the time spent on each activity so that the meeting lasts an hour or an hour and a half. Participants need to decide on the length of each meeting, and the meetings should begin and ending promptly so everyone can schedule accordingly.

In the week following the first meeting, group members may work with the other meditations in Chapter 1. For instance, they may take three days to work with the second meditation and three days for the third, reading and writing a little each day. By the end of those six days it will be time to meet again and start another week of writing exercises.

Suggested Format for Group Meetings

An hour and a half should provide enough time for these meetings. Begin and end at appointed times. The Leader should make a point to arrive ten minutes early to greet members as they arrive.

Gathering and Welcome (5 minutes)

The Leader welcomes the group members and reads aloud the group covenant set at the first meeting.

Lighting of the Christ Candle (1 minute)

The Leader or another group member lights the Christ candle and says one of the following prayers or another prayer that suits the group:

Jesus Christ, be our guide as we read and write with God's Holy Word. Holy Spirit come, illuminate our imagination and nurture us where we are today. Amen.

God, you have given us the abilities to reason, to imagine, and to create. We turn to you now, O God. Fill us with your Spirit. Help us to know ourselves and to know you through Christ Jesus our Lord. Amen.

God of the created world, God of mercy and beauty, let your Word take root in our hearts today and bear the fruits of goodness. Amen.

The Leader or another group member may also choose to write a prayer that fits the personality or feelings of the group.

Reading of Scripture Passage (10-15 minutes)

The Leader may choose one of the three passages in the chapter to read or ask if the participants have a preference.

The Leader will read the passage three times aloud with a short silence between each reading.

Writing Time (30-35 minutes)

The Leader reads aloud the following invitation or one similar:

> If you already have an idea of how you want to write with this scripture, feel free to begin. If not, turn to the reflection questions and possible writing exercises for this scripture. Choose the exercise that sparks your interest and begin writing. Spelling and composition are not important. Write what comes, even if it is a phrase or word over and over. Trust your imagination whether it is moving slowly or flowing rapidly.

Allow silence or simple, soft instrumental music while participants write.

Sharing the Experience (30-35 minutes)

The Leader may share first—reading what he or she has written, talking about the process of writing, or both. The Leader may ask if another group member wants to share first. Allow the sharing to develop on its own as people desire to speak or go around the group asking participants to share.

Prayers of Participants (5 minutes)

The Leader asks participants for prayer concerns. The Leader or another group member closes in prayer noting participants' concerns as well as any concerns for the world or local community and church.

Benediction by Leader (1 minute)

> *The grace of the Lord Jesus Christ, the love of God, and the communion of the Holy Spirit be with you all. Amen.*

For Use in an Established Group

The same format outlined above can be used in a group that already meets. Any of the chapters can be broken up to be used week-by-week without having participants do work on their own during the week. For example, the book could be used over the course of eighteen weeks, using one scripture per week. The book could be used over the course of twelve weeks, with the Leader or group members choosing the scriptures from each chapter to use for each week.

For Two People

Two people can meet to read and write together. For years, I met with a friend to share my writing and reflection process. The two can read and write on their own throughout the week and meet to share their reflections on the process and to pray together. Or the two may want to conduct a full session, as outlined for a small group, taking turns leading.

As a Solitary Practice

You can use this book for a personal practice, adapting the format above. Even if you do not want to use the steps outlined above, I highly recommend structuring your time. At the very least, open and close with prayer. I suggest writing out your prayer each time. Looking back over the prayers you use to open and close your writing time can reveal where you have been and where you may be headed.

A Final Note

God is with you always and will be present in your writing. You may feel a need for someone with whom you can speak honestly and openly about your life. I believe God wants to be that conversation partner; God hears you and speaks to you. This writing practice is just one way you can cultivate a relationship with God, and it is a good one. There may be times you feel your connection to God and times you do not. I encourage you not to worry about this ebb and flow of experience. Have faith in God's caring presence in your life and take note of your writing experience, simply describing it to yourself rather than judging it as good or bad. Have fun. Your writing does not have to be serious, though it probably will be sometimes. The human experience is as much comedy as it is tragedy. If any of the questions arouse a sense of sarcasm or irony, let those feelings influence your writing. When writing in a group, allow the energy of the group to encourage you in your writing, but take care to maintain and appreciate your own voice. Be yourself. I hope this writing process is as helpful to you as it has been to me. I wish you the very best. Happy writing.

CPSIA information can be obtained at www.ICGtesting.com
Printed in the USA
LVOW11s2356160115

423136LV00004B/8/P

9 780835 813754